Empiri Studies of Ego Mechanisms of Defense

Empirical Studies of Ego Mechanisms of Defense

Edited by
George E. Vaillant, M.D.

Raymond Sobel Professor of Psychiatry, Dartmouth Medical School, Hanover, New Hampshire; and Director, Study of Adult Development, Harvard University Health Services, Cambridge, Massachusetts

AMERICAN PSYCHIATRIC PRESS, INC.
Washington, D.C.

Manufactured in the U.S.A.

The paper used in this publication meets the minimum requirements of American National Standard for Information Sciences—Permanence of Paper for Printed Library Materials, ANSI Z39.48-1984.

Library of Congress Cataloging in Publication Data

Main entry under title:

Empirical studies of ego mechanisms of defense.

    (Clinical insights)
    Includes bibliographies.
    1. Defense mechanisms (Psychology) 2. Ego (Psychology)
3. Psychodiagnostics. I. Vaillant, George E., 1934-   . II. Series. [DNLM:
1. Defense Mechanisms. 2. Ego. WM 193 E55]
RC455.4.D43E46 1986   154.2'2   86-1216
ISBN 0-88048-131-5 (alk. paper)

Contents

Contributors

WILLIAM BEARDSLEE, M.D.
*Assistant Professor of Psychiatry, Harvard Medical School;
and Children's Hospital, Boston, Massachusetts*

MICHAEL BOND, M.D.
*Assistant Professor of Psychiatry, McGill University and
Sir Mortimer B. Davis Jewish General Hospital, Montreal, Canada*

ELIZABETH GELFAND, ED.D.
*Research Associate in Psychiatry, Massachusetts Mental Health Center and
Harvard Medical School, Boston, Massachusetts*

STUART HAUSER, M.D., PH.D.
*Associate Professor of Psychiatry, Massachusetts Mental Health Center and
Harvard Medical School, Boston, Massachusetts*

ALAN M. JACOBSON, M.D.
*Associate Professor of Psychiatry, Joslin Diabetes Center and
Harvard Medical School, Boston, Massachusetts*

LEIGH MCCULLOUGH, PH.D.
Research Psychologist, Beth Israel Medical Center, New York, New York

GIL G. NOAM, DIPL. PSYCH.
*Lecturer in Psychology, Harvard Medical School; and Director, Evaluative
Services—Children's Unit, McLean Hospital, Belmont, Massachusetts*

J. CHRISTOPHER PERRY, M.D., M.P.H.
*Assistant Professor of Psychiatry, Cambridge Hospital and Harvard Medical
School, Cambridge, Massachusetts*

SALLY I. POWERS, ED.D.
*Instructor in Psychiatry, Harvard Medical School; and Research Associate,
Henry A. Murray Center, Radcliffe College, Cambridge, Massachusetts*

CAROLINE O. VAILLANT, M.S.S.W.
*Research Social Worker, Dartmouth Medical School,
Hanover, New Hampshire*

GEORGE E. VAILLANT, M.D.
*Raymond Sobel Professor of Psychiatry, Dartmouth Medical School,
Hanover, New Hampshire*

Introduction: A Brief History of Empirical Assessment of Defense Mechanisms

Perhaps Freud's most original contribution to human psychology was his inductive hypothesis that unconscious "defense mechanisms" protect the individual from conflicting ideas and emotions. In delineating the nature of ego mechanisms of defense, Freud not only emphasized that upsetting *affects*, not *ideas*, underlay psychopathology but also suggested that much of what is perceived as psychopathology reflects a potentially healing process.

However, both Freud and his students tended to ignore the importance of differentiating defense mechanisms. It took James Strachey, Freud's final editor, and Freud's daughter Anna, his intellectual heir, to appreciate and to emphasize what Freud did not—the variety and the power of the concept of ego mechanisms of defense.

In 1894 Freud had observed not only that affect could be "dislocated or transposed" from ideas (by the mechanisms that Freud would later call dissociation, repression, and isolation), but that it could be "reattached" to other ideas (by displacement) (1). Over a period of 40 years, Freud went on to outline most of the defense mechanisms that we speak of today. He identified five of their important properties: a) Defenses were major means of managing instinct and affect; b) they were unconscious; c) they were discrete from one another; d) although often the hallmarks of major psychiatric syndromes, defenses were reversible; and, finally, e) defenses could be adaptive as well as pathological. However, general scientific acceptance of defenses has always been in doubt. I believe there are two reasons for this.

Freud's contemporaries, Sherrington and Pavlov, had also observed and defined "unconscious" psychological mechanisms. But from the start, their students had paid full attention to such mechanisms. First, the mechanisms postulated by Sherrington and Pavlov did not deal with emotions; and second, their students had no difficulty demonstrating these postulated mechanisms via empirical studies. In contrast—I suspect because ego mechanisms involve such emotionally charged processes—differentiated defenses have been disavowed by his critics, by Freud himself (2), and even by some of his most recent followers (3). Defenses have also proven extremely resistant to empirical study.

During the first decade after he described them, Freud clearly conceptualized defense mechanisms as distinct from each other. Thus, by 1905 in the single work *Jokes and Their Relation to the Unconscious* (4), Freud described the separate mechanisms of humor, distortion, displacement, repression, suppression, phantasy, and isolation. After 1905, however, the term defense (*abwehr*) no longer figured prominently in Freud's work and was replaced (1906) by " 'repression' (as I now began to say instead of 'defence')" (2, p. 276). For 20 years, the distinction between individual ego mechanisms remained blurred in Freud's writings.

It is no coincidence that Freud's decision to redifferentiate ego mechanisms of defense from nonspecific terms such as "repression" and "countercathexis" occurred simultaneously with the birth of ego psychology. In 1926, in *Inhibitions, Symptoms and Anxiety* (5), Freud formally suggested that the concept of defense be reintroduced as a broad term under which specifically named individual ego mechanisms such as "repression" and "isolation" would be subsumed. He pointed out that the two mechanisms represented very different ways of handling the same affects " . . . I have revived a concept . . . of which I made exclusive use thirty years ago when I first began to study the subject [of anxiety] but which I later abandoned. I refer to the term 'defensive process.' I afterwards replaced it by the word 'repression,' but the relation between the two remained uncertain. It will be an undoubted advantage, I think, to revert to the old concept of 'defence' " (p. 163).

Nevertheless, in 1932 in his *New Introductory Lectures* (6), Freud cited only four defenses as relevant to waking behavior: repression, sublimation, displacement, and reaction formation. Four years later, Freud advised the interested student, "There are an extraordinarily large number of methods (or mechanisms, as we say) used by our ego in the discharge of its defensive functions. . . . my daughter, the child analyst, is writing a book upon them" (7, p. 245). He was referring, of course, to Anna Freud's *The Ego and the Mechanisms of Defense* (8), which to this day remains one of the definitive texts on the subject.

However, Anna Freud only pointed the way to empirical study. First, she did not solve the problem of specificity. For example, by convention Anna Freud is said to have described 10 defense mechanisms. However, not only did she fail to provide mutually exclusive definitions but at least 20 differently labeled defenses can be found in *The Ego and the Mechanisms of Defense*. Second, Anna Freud admitted that the "chronology of psychic processes (defenses) is still one of the most obscure fields of analytic theory" (8).

Only as we learn to differentiate defensive processes from each other can we understand our patients' choice of symptoms and appreciate the hierarchical development of the ego and its functions. But to construct such a developmental continuum of defenses requires rater reliability, and methodological difficulty in this area hampered the efforts of Anna Freud and her Hampstead co-workers to uncover the developmental sequence of defense mechanisms. In spite of the ambitious goals of the Hampstead Index (9) in systematically cataloguing the defenses of children in psychoanalysis, no substantive empirical publications on defenses have emerged from The Hampstead (now Anna Freud) Clinic.

Many contributors to ego psychology (for example, Glover, Brenner, Gill, and Rapaport) recognized the likelihood of a hierarchical continuum of defenses from pathological to less pathological, but they did not provide specific outlines or empirical underpinnings. The closest that Anna Freud ever came was in the mid-1960s, when she wrote, "Defenses have their own chronology ... they are more apt to have pathological results if they come into use before the appropriate age or are kept up too long after it. Examples are denial and projection, which are 'normal' in early childhood and lead to pathology in later years; or repression and reaction formation, which cripple the child's personality if used too early" (9, p. 177).

Clearly, recognition of hierarchically differentiated defenses requires a highly developed appreciation of the healthy ego. Freud and his early followers had chosen to study children and psychologically impaired individuals; they paid relatively less attention to the fate of a given defense as the child matured and as the patient recovered. However, differentiated mechanisms of defense become clearest when one can study the psychopathology of everyday life in detail, and it was not until World War II that psychoanalytically trained researchers began to study healthy adaptation in normal populations.

A complete list of the influential postwar clinical investigators would be much too long for inclusion here, but Percival Symonds, Ernst Kris, George Engel, Robert White, David Hamburg, Irving Janis, Lois Murphy, and Karl Menninger belong on the list of those who deserve credit for underscoring the need to define a hierarchy of defense mechanisms. Every one of these investigators, however, presented a different nomenclature and a different schema for assessing defenses. None of them provided mutually exclusive definitions, sought rater reliability, or provided empirical evidence beyond clinical anecdote.

After the war there also arose a parallel experimental literature on defenses, but it was based in the psychology laboratory and not the clinic. Exhaustive reviews by Moos (10), Coelho et al. (11), and Kline (12) have summarized findings from several hundred studies. In contrast to clinical investigations, these studies achieved definition, rater reliability, assessment strategy, and at times even consensual validation. But the price paid for reliability and experimental control was results that had very limited relevance to real life. The controlled setting of the psychology laboratory, the uniform stimuli of the pencil and paper tests, and the revealing insights from projective tests failed to provide any systematic basis for understanding defenses in the real world. Validity was sacrificed for reliability.

Thus, if the clinical studies were unsatisfactory methodologically, so the methodological studies were unsatisfactory clinically. For example, in a sample of 100 nonpatient college graduates, I contrasted their defensive style in everyday life with defenses identified from results obtained by rating their responses to Thematic Apperception Tests. There was no correlation! By way of less anecdotal evidence, Kline summarized his review of the experimental literature: "It is clear from our discussion of the empirical studies reported in this chapter that methodological difficulties, not unexpectedly, have proved too much for most investigators" (12, p. 192).

One of the most ambitious, important, and illustrative research studies during this period was the 1964 investigation by Carl Wolff, Myron Hofer, and John Mason on the relationship between psychological defenses and urinary corticoid excretion rate in the parents of fatally ill children (13). Their work illustrated the problems of specificity and reliability in assessing defenses, which crippled investigators in one of the most sophisticated stress laboratories in the country.

In the 1960s an important advance came through the longitudinal studies by both Norma Haan, a psychologist at the Institute of Human Development (IHD) at Berkeley, and Elvin Semrad, a professor of psychiatry at the Massachusetts Mental Health Center at Harvard Medical School. In 1963 Norma Haan described 20 adaptive styles with explicit definitions (most unusual in the literature up to that time) (14). These styles were divided into two groups: 10 styles were described as coping (healthy), and 10 adaptive styles—"first cousins" to the other 10—were described as defending (pathological). On the basis of interview notes obtained after an average of 12 hours of interviewing, two IHD raters judged 99 members of the Oakland Growth Studies for Haan's coping/defending styles. The value of Haan's work was that it explicitly defined a hierarchy of defenses according to pathological impact, tried to provide mutually exclusive definitions, and then tried to demonstrate the validity of the scheme by correlating her results with important, longitudinally derived measures of mental health. Haan's efforts have spawned a number of empirical studies, many of which are summarized in her book *Coping and Defending* (15).

Two limitations of Haan's study were that her data base reflected a unique longitudinal study, and some of her definitions of defenses were idiosyncratic. A third limitation was rater reliability. Haan measured interrater reliability on all of the 20 mechanisms for both men and women. Rater reliabilities for seven of her mechanisms were less than .4.

Simultaneously, Elvin Semrad also studied defenses in a developmental longitudinal context through scrutiny of the recovery process in acute schizophrenia. Semrad outlined a finite list of defenses arranged hierarchically (16) and also stimulated empirical studies by a number of his residents. In 1973 both Semrad and co-workers (17) and Leopold Bellak and his co-workers (18) reported attempts to develop an ego profile scale as a means of studying schizophrenia. Neither rating scale has ever been adequately validated.

Thus, by the mid-1970s the empirical understanding of defense mechanisms remained in semantic and conceptual disarray. This disarray was clearly illustrated by a meeting held at the New York State Psychiatric Institute in the fall of 1977, at which I was present, to plan for the *Diagnostic and Statistical Manual of Mental Disorders, Third Edition (DSM-III)*. A group of psychoanalysts with a commitment to developing defenses as a possible axis for *DSM-III* met with Robert Spitzer to discuss the justification of such a step. After meeting for several hours it became clear that we were unable to agree of a common list of defenses, on consensually based definitions, or on the pathological implications of certain defenses. Each member had a different view of what constituted an important set of defenses. There appeared to be an inadequate empirical framework on which to build consensus and resolve disagreement. For that reason, among others, the decision was made not to include defenses in *DSM-III*.

Table 1. Correlation of Selected Defense Mechanisms With Global Assessment of Mental Health

		INVESTIGATOR			
Term from *Comprehensive Textbook of Psychiatry**	Haan (15)	Vaillant (20)	Battista (23)	Vaillant (21)	Bond (25)
I. Mature Defenses					
Anticipation (objectivity)**	coping	++	+	++	not rated
Suppression (suppression, concentration)	coping	++	+	++	+
Altruism	coping	n.s.	n.s.	++	not rated
Sublimation (substitution, sublimation)	coping	n.s.	+	++	+
Humor (playfulness)	coping	not rated	not rated	++	+
Asceticism	not rated	not rated	not rated	not rated	
II. Neurotic (Intermediate) Defenses					
Intellectualization (isolation)	defending	n.s.	+	n.s.	n.s.
Repression (repression)	defending	n.s.	n.s.	n.s.	n.s.
Reaction formation (reaction formation)	defending	n.s.	not rated	n.s.	n.s.
Displacement	defending	n.s.	n.s.	+	n.s.
Externalization, inhibition, sexualization, somatization, controlling, rationalization	not rated	not rated	not rated	not rated	
III. Immature Defenses					
Passive aggression or masochism (repression)	defending	n.s.	n.s.	−−	−
Hypochondriasis	not rated	n.s.	n.s.	−−	not rated
Acting out	not rated	−	n.s.	−−	−
Dissociation (denial)	defending	n.s.	−	−−	−
Projection (projection)	defending	−	n.s.	−−	−
Schizoid fantasy	not rated	−	−	−−	not rated
Blocking, introjection, regression	not rated	not rated	not rated	not rated	

n.s. Not significantly correlated with mental health.

* Psychotic or "narcissistic" defenses—for example, denial of external reality, delusional thinking, distortion (hallucinations), that is, mechanisms associated with frank psychosis—have been excluded.

** Terms in parentheses are Haan's terms for equivalent mental processes.

+ or − Positive or negative correlation $p < .05$ (Pearson Product–Moment coefficient) or $r > .25$.

++ or −− Positive or negative correlation $p < .001$.

Table 1 summarizes progress since 1977. It depicts the hierarchy of defenses defined and given wide currency by Kaplan and Sadock's *Modern Synopsis of Psychiatry/3* (19); the same hierarcy is reproduced in part II in the Appendix. The Table demonstrates the general agreement of five recent studies, each of which correlated defensive style with a different measure of mental health.

In a sample of 95 college men followed for several decades, I observed that "mature" defenses correlated positively and "immature" defenses correlated negatively with a 32-item scale reflecting objective success in working and loving (20). Using an inner-city sample of 307 47-year-old men, I replicated the findings (21). The means of assessing mental health was Luborsky's Health Sickness Rating Scale (22); the methodology is described in Chapter 5. Battista (23) assessed the defensive style of 78 psychiatric inpatients by means of an ego function inventory rated on a 5-point Likert scale. He rated the patients' outcome by means of the Global Assessment Scale (24). Bond et al. (25) used a self-administered questionnaire of self-perception of defensive style to 209 patients and nonpatients. Factor analysis revealed four clusters of defenses, which Bond correlated with independent questionnaire measures of ego adaptation and Loevinger's (26) Sentence Completion Test of ego maturity (see Chapter 1 of this monograph). Questions reflecting projection, passive aggression, dissociation, and acting out all loaded highly in the cluster that correlated most negatively with estimates of ego strength and maturity. Questions reflecting humor, suppression, and sublimation all loaded highly in the cluster that correlated most positively with estimates of ego strength and ego maturity. Haan demonstrated that equivalent— but differently labeled—mechanisms, which she called "coping," were significantly correlated with upward social mobility, adult increases in IQ, and three other measures of positive midlife outcome (15). Mechanisms that she called "defending" were negatively correlated with such outcomes.

In summary, the so-called immature defenses in the Table correspond to those inferred intrapsychic mechanisms commonly observed in personality disorders (27), in adolescents, and in the Axis II disorders of *DSM-III*. They are consistently and negatively

correlated with global assessment of mental health. They profoundly distort the affective component of interpersonal relationships. In contrast, the so-called mature defenses correspond to
inferred intrapsychic mechanisms that have been consistently
associated with successful psychological adaptation. These mechanisms allow the individual to experience the affective component
of interpersonal relationships but in a tempered fashion. The
intermediate defenses reflect mechanisms posited by psychoanalytic theory to identify neuroses. Across studies they showed
mixed positive and negative correlations of minimal significance.

The following chapters build on the significant progress that
has already been made toward providing an empirical basis for
defense mechanisms. First, a consensually acceptable glossary of
defenses seems within grasp. Second, modest empirical validation
of such a hierarchical arrangement of defenses seems possible. Still
missing, however, is a solution to the problem of reliable identification of inferred defense mechanisms.

Clearly, one can search for what one seeks where the light is
good, or one can search for what one seeks where one thinks it
may be hidden. Those who have sought to search for defense
mechanisms where the methodological light is brightest, with
psychological instruments and in the laboratory, have found good
light but little of clinical value. The following chapters present
fresh efforts to seek defenses where they exist—in the real world.

The monograph is interdisciplinary in its approach to defenses.
All of the investigators are clinicians. In addition, Hauser brings to
his work the special interests of the psychoanalyst and the developmental psychologist, Perry the interests of the epidemiologist,
McCullough those of the behavioral psychologist, Bond those of a
psychometrician, Jacobson those of the medical clinician, and I,
those of a devout follower of Adolf Meyer and Erikson.

Among the obvious problems to be addressed in this monograph are how to separate symptom from defense, how to increase
poor rater reliability, how to specify rules of inference in order to
create mutually exclusive definitions, and how to keep raters'

countertransference and projection from biasing clinical assessment of subjects' defenses.

One way of bringing empirical order to procedures for rating defenses is to apply more than one methodology to the same clinical sample. We cannot measure a mountain from top to bottom, but we can assess its height through triangulation, by integrating two indirect and oblique views of its peak. So it is with defenses. As with the generalizations made in cautious psychobiography, defenses can be identified by combining biography, autobiography, and the subject's symptoms or creative products. Defenses can also be identified by sheer redundancy, as illustrated in McCullough's chapter. Defenses can be identified by using both rated interviews and self-reported response to stress, as in Perry's chapter, and defenses can be identified by combining pencil and paper self-report instruments with the clinical interview as described in Chapter 5.

As has already been mentioned, semantics has been a major problem in the experimental study of defenses. Clearly, there are as many defenses as there are colors in the spectrum. To help in bringing order to the field, this monograph includes five glossaries of defenses in the Appendix. The purpose is to allow future investigators to compare and weigh the merits and problems of competing definitions and rating schemes. In this way, the monograph is designed to help move the field toward standard definitions.

Clearly, all the pieces are not yet in place. There is no question that defenses, perhaps like subatomic particles, can be studied only with great difficulty and expense. But understanding, appreciating, and even measuring defenses may be central to the study of psychopathology. It is in that spirit that defenses are being tentatively included in *DSM-III(R)*. It is hoped that this monograph will assist those attempting to assess and study defenses in the future.

George E. Vaillant, M.D.

References

1. Freud S: The neuro-psychoses of defense (1894), in The Complete Psychological Works, vol. 3. Translated by Strachey J. London, Hogarth Press, 1962

2. Freud S: My views on the part played by sexuality in the aetiology of the neuroses (1906), in The Complete Psychological Works, vol. 7. Translated by Strachey J. London, Hogarth Press, 1953

3. Brenner C: Defense and defense mechanisms. Psychoanal Q 50:557-569, 1981

4. Freud S: Jokes and their relation to the unconscious (1905), in The Complete Psychological Works, vol. 8. Translated by Strachey J. London, Hogarth Press, 1960

5. Freud S: Inhibitions, symptoms and anxiety (1926), in The Complete Psychological Works, vol. 20. Translated by Strachey J. London, Hogarth Press, 1959

6. Freud S: New introductory lectures (1932), in The Complete Psychological Works, vol. 22. Translated by Strachey J. London, Hogarth Press, 1964

7. Freud S: A disturbance of memory on the Acropolis (1936), in The Complete Psychological Works, vol. 22. Translated by Strachey J. London, Hogarth Press, 1964

8. Freud A: The Ego and the Mechanisms of Defense (1937). New York, International Universities Press, 1966

9. Freud A: Normality and Pathology in Childhood: Assessments of Development. New York, International Universities Press, 1965

10. Moos RH: Psychosocial techniques in the assessment of adaptive behavior, in Coping and Adaptation. Edited by Coelho GV, Hamburg DA, Adams JE. New York, Basic Books, 1974

11. Coelho GV, Hamburg DA, Adams JE: Coping and Adaptation. New York, Basic Books, 1974

12. Kline P: Fact and Fantasy in Freudian Theory. London, Methuen, 1972

13. Wolff CT, Friedman SB, Hofer MA, et al: Relationship between psychosocial defenses and mean urinary 17–hydroxycorticoid excretion rates, I: a predictive study of parents of fatally ill children. Psychosom Med 26:576-591, 1964

14. Haan N: Proposed model of ego functioning: coping and defense mechanisms in relationship to IQ change. Psychological Monographs 77:1-23, 1963

15. Haan N: Coping and Defending. San Francisco, Jossey-Bass, 1977

16. Semrad EV: The organization of ego defenses and object loss, in The Loss of Loved Ones. Edited by Moriarty DM. Springfield, IL, Charles C Thomas, 1967

17. Semrad EV, Grinspoon L, Feinberg SE: Development of an ego profile scale. Arch Gen Psychiatry 28:70-77, 1963

18. Bellak L, Hurvich M, Gediman HK: Ego Functions in Schizophrenics, Neurotics, and Normals. New York, John Wiley & Sons, 1973

19. Kaplan HI, Sadock BJ: Modern Synopsis of Comprehensive Textbook of Psychiatry/III. Baltimore, Williams and Wilkins, 1981

20. Vaillant GE: Adaptation to Life. Boston, Little, Brown, 1977

21. Vaillant GE: An empirically derived hierarchy of adaptive mechanisms and its usefulness as a potential diagnostic axis. Acta Psychiatr Scand (Suppl 319) 71:171-180, 1985

22. Luborsky L: Clinicians' judgments of mental health. Arch Gen Psychiatry 7:407-417, 1962

23. Battista JR: Empirical test of Vaillant's hierarchy of ego functions. Am J Psychiatry 139:356-357, 1982

24. Endicott J, Spitzer RL, Fleiss JL, et al: The Global Assessment Scale: a procedure for measuring overall severity of psychiatric disturbance. Arch Gen Psychiatry 33:766-771, 1976

25. Bond M, Gardner ST, Christian J, et al: Empirical study of self-rated defense styles. Arch Gen Psychiatry 40:333-338, 1983

26. Loevinger J: Ego Development. San Francisco, Jossey-Bass, 1976

27. Millon T: Disorders of Personality. New York, John Wiley & Sons, 1981

1

An Empirical Study of Defense Styles

Michael Bond, M.D.

1

An Empirical Study of Defense Styles

The concept of defense mechanisms has been a clinically useful metaphor to explain certain speculated intrapsychic processes. However, the accurate empirical measurement of defense mechanisms has been confounded by lack of interrater reliability, validity, and conceptual clarity. In March 1983, I, along with Susan T. Gardner, Ph.D., John Christian, Ph.D., and John Sigal, Ph.D., reported on our research with a defense style questionnaire designed to eliminate the problem of interrater reliability (1). In a follow-up study, with Jacqueline Sagala Vaillant, M.D., we reported our findings on the relationship between defense style and diagnosis (2). Currently I am trying to establish validity of the defense style questionnaire by comparing the results of patients' self-reports with raters' judgments of defense mechanisms while watching videotaped clinical interviews. This chapter brings together all our research to date.

The concept of defense mechanisms is pervasive in the psychi-

Adapted from: Bond M, Gardner ST, Christian J, et al: Empirical study of self-rated defense styles. Arch Gen Psychiatry 40:333-338, March 1983 (copyright 1983, American Medical Association); and Bond M, Sagala Vaillant J: An empirical study of the relationship between diagnosis and defense styles. Arch Gen Psychiatry (in press). Portions of these articles have been reprinted by permission of the American Medical Association.

atric and psychoanalytic literature, but there is confusion and inconsistency about what defense mechanisms are and how they relate to diagnosis. Laplanche and Pontalis (3) defined defense mechanisms as follows:

> ... different types of operations through which defense may be given specific expression. Which of these mechanisms predominate in a given case depends upon the type of illness under consideration, upon the developmental stage reached, upon the extent to which the defensive conflict has been worked out, and so on.
>
> It is generally agreed that the ego puts the defense mechanism to use, but the theoretical question of whether their mobilization always presupposes the existence of an organized ego capable of sustaining them is an open one. (p. 109)

Laplanche and Pontalis then went on to say, "Freud's choice of the word mechanism is intended, from the outset, to indicate the fact that psychical phenomena are so organized as to permit scientific observation and analysis" (p. 109). However, the scientific examination of defense mechanisms has proved to be a difficult and confused exercise. Our primary purpose was to develop a questionnaire for the experimental study of defense mechanisms that did not rely on the rater's subjective judgment. Our achievement was more modest. We devised a self-administered questionnaire that taps possible conscious derivatives of defense mechanisms.

Within the definition of Laplanche and Pontalis, one can see some of the confusing facets of defense mechanisms associated both with "illness" and with "an organized ego capable of sustaining them." These mechanisms can be seen both as a constricting influence that limits growth and as an adaptive process that protects the person and enables him or her to function. This theme runs through the writing of Freud (4), A. Freud (5), and Kernberg (6), even as they link defense mechanisms with illness. Vaillant (7), Haan et al. (8), and Semrad et al. (9) are more explicit in describing the adaptive aspects of defense or coping mechanisms as well as the regressive aspects. We wanted to investigate whether there is "an intimate connection between special forms of defense and particular illnesses," as Freud suggested (4, pp. 163-164), or whether there is a factor other than specific illnesses that is more closely correlated with specific groupings of defense mechanisms.

This focus brought us to certain crucial questions: Which phenomena can be labelled defense or coping mechanisms? Can these phenomena be measured? Do defense or coping mechanisms cluster into defense styles? Can defenses be measured? Along with function are defense styles organized? Can defense styles be related to the developmental stage reached or other unique information about ego functioning?

DEFENSE MECHANISMS

To answer the first question—regarding which phenomena can be called defenses—we began with Freud (4), who listed regression, repression, reaction formation, isolation, undoing, projection, introjection, turning against the self, and reversal. A. Freud (5) described sublimation, displacement, denial in fantasy, denial in word and act, identification with the aggressor, and altruism. Kernberg (6) and Klein (10) described splitting, omnipotence with devaluation, primitive idealization, projective identification, and psychotic denial.

Vaillant (7) substituted some overt behaviors for intrapsychic processes in his study, claiming that "such substitution permits the examination of ego function in operational rather than in theoretical terms" (p. 541). In so doing, he added to the list of defenses fantasy, passive aggression, hypochondriasis, acting out, suppression, humor, and anticipation.

It seems timely to try to bring some order into such a bewildering array of proposed defenses. We proposed to see whether current statistical methods—specifically, factor analysis—could serve this purpose.

Several investigations have attempted to answer the question of whether and how these phenomena can be measured. In trying to develop an experimental method for the study of defense mechanisms, both Vaillant (7) and Haan et al. (8) used psychiatric interviews in combination with other measures, such as psychological tests, questionnaires, and autobiographical reports. Vaillant pointed out that the clinical judgment required in his study limited the objectivity and reliability of the ratings. He went on to emphasize the need to make intrapsychic processes operational so that defenses can be studied experimentally.

Bellak et al. (11) attempted to determine empirically the extent to which defense mechanisms in general maladaptively affect ideation, behavior, and the adaptive level of other ego functions, and the extent to which defenses succeed or fail in controlling dysphoric affects. The difficulty with this approach is that it did not provide a means for identifying and examining individual defense mechanisms.

Semrad et al. (9) created an ego profile scale that empirically measured different types of ego functioning. The items for the questionnaire were generated by two of the authors and then categorized into nine ego defense categories by 25 senior psychiatrists. An item was accepted as indicative of a particular ego defense if a sufficient number of raters independently agreed on its assignment to that category. The ego profile scale was filled out by patients' therapists on a weekly basis. The creation of this scale, as well as the scoring of the scale, depended solely on therapists' opinions and observations. An instrument that does not depend on therapists' subjective opinions for predetermining defense grouping or for making individual ratings is still needed.

MEASUREMENT OF DEFENSE MECHANISMS

The problem of measuring intrapsychic phenomena that are often unconscious is immense. The method that we developed for this study is merely an attempt to approach the measurement of defense mechanisms through self-appraisals of conscious derivatives. Although this method does not directly measure defense mechanisms, it may relate to them.

In this chapter, the term *defense mechanism* is used to describe not only an unconscious intrapsychic process but also behavior that is either consciously or unconsciously designed to reconcile internal drive with external demands. It would be impossible to conclude anything about isolated defense mechanisms, but we hoped that we could approximate the measurement of groups of defense mechanisms that we call *defense style.*

We hypothesized that defense styles might identify aspects of a person's stage of development and render other information about ego functioning independent of diagnosis. Vaillant (7, 12), who divided defenses into narcissistic, immature, neurotic, and mature groups, demonstrated that this theoretical hierarchy of defenses correlated with empirical definitions of mental health. Haan et al. (8) and Haan (13) divided ego processes into coping, defensive, and fragmentation, placing emphasis on different styles and not only on level of development. Semrad et al. (9) also proposed a hierarchy of ego functioning, specifically with regard to defense styles.

Shapiro (14) used neurotic styles to refer to "a form or mode of functioning . . . that is identifiable, in an individual, through a range of his specific acts." He outlined four major neurotic styles: obsessive–compulsive, hysterical, paranoid, and impulsive, but used no empirical data.

Linking defenses with specific illnesses can create confusion. Defense should refer to a style of dealing with conflict or stress, whereas diagnosis should refer to a constellation of symptoms and signs. Separating the examination of defenses from the issue of diagnosis would allow the use of the concept of defense more precisely during investigation of fluctuations in a person's style in dealing with a particular stress at a particular time and under particular circumstances; the use of that style would also reveal something about the level of that psychosocial development.

A description follows of our preliminary attempt to contribute to the search for an objective, empirical method of studying the relations among defense mechanisms, diagnosis, level of maturity, and other ongoing psychological phenomena.

SUBJECTS AND METHODS

Subjects

In our study, 209 volunteers participated, 111 nonpatients and 98 patients. The persons in the nonpatient sample, from their own point of view, were functioning adequately and at the time of testing were not undergoing psychiatric treatment. The patient sample consisted of 98 persons drawn from the psychiatric wards or psychiatric outpatient departments of three university teaching or affiliated hospitals.

The nonpatient sample comprised 10 high school students, five students at a junior college, 36 university students, 56 subjects actively employed in socially recognized occupations or as home-makers, and three retired persons. Ages ranged from 16 to 69 years (mean, 31 years); 48 of the subjects were male and 63 were female.

The patient sample included 42 inpatients and 56 outpatients. According to the simple, forced-choice evaluation sheet, the following diagnoses were made by the attending psychologist or psychiatrist: psychotic, 39; borderline, 26; neurotic, 22; personality disorder, 6; and other, 5. Ages ranged from 25 to 64 years (mean, 27 years); 48 were male and 50 were female. The mean ages in the three major diagnostic categories of psychotic, borderline, and neurotic were 29.3 (SD, 11.2), 25.1 (SD, 7.3), and 24.0 (SD, 11.4) years, respectively.

Methods

Questionnaire Measuring Self-report of Defensive Styles. In the classical psychoanalytic sense, defense mechanisms are an unconscious process. A self-report thus may not detect a phenomenon of which a subject is unaware. Our approach to this objection was based on the following premises. There are times when defenses fail temporarily, and at those times subjects may become aware of their unacceptable impulses and their usual styles of defending against them. In addition, others often point out defense mechanisms to the person. A statement such as, "People tell me that I often take my anger out on someone other than the one at whom I'm really angry," might tap displacement even if the subject is unaware of defensive behavior at the time that it is happening. A statement such as, "When I have a close friend, I need to be with him all the time," can tap clinging behavior because the subject may have had this behavior pointed out to him or her, or the subject may have noted anxious or depressed feelings when unable to use this defensive behavior. The questionnaire was designed to elicit manifestations of a subject's characteristic style of dealing with conflict, either conscious or unconscious, based on the assumption that persons can accurately comment on their behavior from a distance. Only a clinical examination could identify unconscious processes as they are happening.

With this rationale, statements were designed to reflect behavior suggestive of the following 24 defense or coping mechanisms: acting out, pseudoaltruism, as-if behavior, clinging, humor, passive–aggressive behavior, regression, somatization, suppression, withdrawal, dissociation, denial, displacement, omnipotence–devaluation, inhibition, intellectualization, identification, primitive idealization, projection, reaction formation, repression, splitting, sublimation, and turning against self. These statements were subjected to an initial test of face validity by asking two psychologists and one psychiatrist (two of the three are psychoanalysts), independently, to match up each statement with its relevant defense or coping mechanism. Only the statements on which they all could agree formed our initial 97-statement questionnaire.

The full revised questionnaire can be found in part VI of the Appendix. Below are some representative examples:

1. "If someone mugged me and stole my money, I'd rather he be helped than punished" (reaction formation).
2. "There's no such thing as finding a little good in everyone. If you're bad, you're all bad" (splitting).
3. "If my boss bugged me, I might make a mistake in my work or work more slowly so as to get back at him" (passive–aggressive behavior).
4. "I always feel that someone I know is like a guardian angel" (primitive idealization).

Subjects were asked to indicate their degree of agreement or disagreement with each statement on a 9-point scale: 1 indicated strong disagreement and 9 indicated strong agreement. All scales were constructed so that a high score on any one defense measure indicated that subject was using that defense.

In a pilot project, we tested 30 patients on the first version of our questionnaire, which consisted of the statements measuring self-appraisal of defense style randomly interspersed with statements from a parallel research project (R. D. Brown, M.D., and S. T. Gardner, Ph.D., personal communication, Jan 15, 1980) designed to measure ego functioning. Internal consistency among statements designed to measure the same defense was assessed through item-to-total correlations. Only statements correlating with their parent group at a significance level of greater than .001 were retained. (The number of statements in each category ranged from one to six. Thus, the item-to-total correlation procedure is satisfactory for only some of the defenses. The face validity criterion mentioned earlier can be considered a complement, for item selection purposes, to the item-to-total correlation method when the latter would yield spuriously high correlations.) On this basis, we retained 81 of the initial 97 statements measuring possible conscious derivatives of defense mechanisms and have added seven statements more.

Our hypotheses were that 1) factor analysis would demonstrate separate clusters of defense mechanisms—that is, defensive styles, and 2) defenses thought to be immature (such as acting out, projection, withdrawal, and passive–aggressive behavior) would cluster at the opposite end from defenses thought to be more mature.

(This approach differs from that of Semrad et al. (9) in that it does not cluster defenses into preconceived categories; it relies on factor analysis to determine the clusters. The approach also differs from that of Semrad et al. in that the data come from subjects' responses to a questionnaire rather than clinicians' ratings.)

Ego Development.   The following measures of ego development were correlated with the data from the defense questionnaire to determine if there was a hierarchy of defense mechanisms.

Ego Function Questionnaire.   In an attempt to cross-validate Bellak et al.'s (11) conclusions that ego functioning is multidimensional, Brown and Gardner (personal communication) constructed a questionnaire designed to measure a number of different ego functions. Since only one factor was found, Brown and Gardner argued that a subject's total score on the questionnaire, which is referred to as the "ego strength score," reflected the person's general level of adaptation.

Sentence Completion Test of Loevinger. The second measure of ego development was a sentence completion test that consisted of 36 stems: 23 from Loevinger (15) and Loevinger and Wessler (16) and 13 from Aronoff (17). Subjects completed items in whatever way they wished. Two of Loevinger and Wessler's original raters rated one third of the Loevinger protocols according to the Loevinger–Wessler method of rating. The interrater reliability coefficient was .84 ($p < .001$). The remaining protocols were scored by one rater. Ego development scores computed on the basis of the sentence completion test are referred to herein as the "ego development score."

Several questions can be raised concerning the validity of Loevinger and Wessler's sentence completion test. First is the question of discriminant validity—whether the test is measuring qualities or characteristics that are different from those measured by other tests. Because several criteria for scoring the test concern cognitive differentiation or complexity, it is important to establish that the test is not simply measuring intelligence or IQ level. Blasi (18) reported correlations of between .46 and .50 between scores on the sentence completion test and the Large–Thorndike intelligence test. Thus, only 21 to 25 percent of ego development level variance is accounted for by IQ.

Second, there is the question of predictive validity—that is, how effective the test is in predicting an external criterion. Hauser (19) argued that while a single external criterion would be unlikely to be related to any particular ego development stage, patterns or constellations of behavior should serve as suitable criteria. In this regard Cox (2) considered helping behavior in relation to ego development, Blasi (21) considered responsibility, and Hoppe (22) looked at conformity behavior in relation to ego development. Findings are generally extremely complex, frequently because situational cues were not adequately taken into account.

Finally, a closely related question is one that concerns construct validity—that is, if the construct of ego development (23) is accurate, then certain phenomena should be expected to follow. Hauser (19) has reviewed the numerous phenomena that may be related to the construct, but a few basic assumptions about interpersonal behavior can be mentioned here. For instance, Frank and Quinlan (24) reported that subjects who scored at the lower ego developmental levels (impulsive and self-protective) showed significantly ($p < .05$) more fighting incidents and running away than adolescents from all other stages. Blasi (21) found that the relation between the degree to which sixth-grade boys and girls behaved responsibly (rated by these observers) and their ego development scores was statistically significant, the correlation being .56 for girls and .54 for boys.

The Loevinger–Wessler (16) conception of ego development postulates that the tendency to conform increases through the early stages (impulsive and self-protective), peaks at the middle stages (conformist), and declines with later development (conscientious, autonomous, and integrated). Using a variety of techniques, Hoppe (22) rated conformity behaviors and found the predicted relationship: maximum values of conformity were associated with subjects scoring high in the conformist range of the ego development test ($p < .05$).

Although some of Loevinger's basic postulates, such as the invariant sequence of stages, have yet to be thoroughly investigated, an increasing body of research suggests that the sentence completion test is based on a construct that is basically sound and relates well with the constellations of behavior that are described by or can be inferred from Loevinger's account of each stage.

RESULTS

As in the pilot project, item-to-total correlations were carried out for each question, and then for the total score of the questions attributed to each defense mechanism in relation to the factor to which it belonged, to ensure that reliability had been retained and that the statements still correlated with the other statements in

the relevant defense category. All correlations remained significant at a greater than .001 level.

Principal component (type PA1, quartimax rotation) (25, pp.
484-485) factor analyses were carried out on the sets of statements
on the 24 postulated defenses for the entire sample and for the
patient and nonpatient samples taken separately. The size of the
eigen-values indicated that a four-factor solution provided an adequate representation of the data for the combined group and for
the nonpatient and patient samples taken separately. (See Table 1;
other data obtainable on request.) In the factor analysis carried out
on the combined group, and in that on the nonpatient and patient
samples taken separately, the same defenses clustered together.

Table 1. Factor Loadings on Defenses (Combined Sample)*

Defense	Factor 1	Factor 2	Factor 3	Factor 4
Acting out	.76	.11	−.10	−.23
Regression	.67	−.01	−.09	−.29
Passive-aggressive behavior	.74	.10	−.02	−.09
Withdrawal	.75	−.17	.11	.05
Projection	.69	.31	.02	−.41
Inhibition	.69	−.20	.17	−.01
Omnipotence–devaluation	.17	.70	−.10	.21
Splitting	.38	.60	−.05	−.20
Primitive idealization	.36	.54	.36	.15
Pseudoaltruism	.33	−.08	.62	.06
Reaction formation	.36	−.07	.56	.06
Sublimation	−.09	.12	.17	.64
Humor	−.14	.02	−.27	.63
Suppression	−.10	.02	.00	.62
As-if behavior	.62	.05	.07	.32
Clinging	.64	.34	.04	.02
Denial	.33	.04	.52	−.05
Displacement	.49	.15	−.19	.05
Dissociation	.63	.22	.15	−.17
Identification	.45	.32	.19	.29
Intellectualization	.49	−.12	−11	.33
Repression	.53	−.08	.05	−.17
Somatization	.56	.19	.11	.10
Turning against self	.61	−.26	.02	−.03

*Type PAI, quartimax rotation (25).
Reprinted from Bond M, Gardner ST, Christian J, et al: Empirical study of self-rated defense
styles. Arch Gen Psychiatry 40:333-338, March 1983. Copyright 1983 by the American
Medical Association. Reprinted by permission.

Table 2. Intercorrelations of Defense Styles

	Style 2	Style 3	Style 4
Style 1	.39*	.37*	−.28*
Style 2	...	.18**	.07
Style 3	...	...	−.02

*p < .001.
**p < .01.

Defense style 1 (factor 1) consisted of apparent derivatives of defense mechanisms usually viewed as immature, namely, withdrawal, regression, acting out, inhibition, passive aggression, and projection. All of the above produced factor loadings greater than .65 on the combined analyses and greater than .55 on the separate analyses, except for regression, which only loaded at .40 for the nonpatients.

Defense style 2 (factor 2) consisted of apparent derivatives of omnipotence, splitting, and primitive idealization. All three defenses loaded greater than .50 on all three of the factor analyses.

Defense style 3 (factor 3) consisted of apparent derivatives of only two defense mechanisms: reaction formation and pseudo-altruism. There was some question as to whether to include denial within defense style 3, since it loaded fairly highly on both the factor analysis of the combined sample and that of the patient sample taken separately. However, denial was eliminated because it loaded negatively on this factor when the analysis was carried out on the nonpatient sample alone.

Defense style 4 (factor 4) consisted of apparent derivatives of suppression, sublimation, and humor, all of which loaded at a greater than .50 level on all three factor analyses, with the exception of sublimation, which loaded at the .47 level when factoring was done on the nonpatient sample alone.

Projection showed a strong negative loading on factor 4 for the patient sample, whereas regression had a strong negative loading on factor 4 for the nonpatient population.

The level of development of these four defense styles was as-

Table 3. Correlations of Defense Styles With Loevinger's Ego Development
(15) and Ego Strength Measures of Brown and Gardner

	Style 1	Style 2	Style 3	Style 4
Ego strength	−.91*	−.37*	−.38*	.32*
Loevinger's ego development	−.42*	−.22	−.29**	.19**

*$p < .001$.
**$p < .01$.

Reprinted from Bond M, Gardner ST, Christian J, et al: Empirical study of self-rated defense
styles. Arch Gen Psychiatry 40:333-338, March 1983. Copyright 1983 by the American
Medical Association. Reprinted by permission.

sessed in a number of ways. Table 2 shows that defense style 1 has
a significant negative correlation with style 4. Table 3 shows the
correlations of the four defense styles with the two measures of
maturity, namely, ego strength score and ego development score.
The relative relations of these correlations indicate that defense
styles 1 through 4 can be ranked in that order—that is, the ego
strength score has a high negative correlation with style 1, a lower
negative correlation with styles 2 and 3, and a significantly positive correlation with style 4. The same pattern holds for the ego
development score (the Loevinger test).

When the ego strength and ego development scores were factor
analyzed (type PAI, quartimax rotation) (25) along with the separate defenses that constitute the four defense styles, a four-factor
solution resulted, with the ego strength and ego development
scores loading negatively with style 1 defenses and positively with
style 4 defenses.

The mean scores on defense styles 1 through 3 are higher for
the patients than the nonpatients (132.7 v 9.7, 36.9 v 30.3, and 25.8
v 22.6), whereas the score on defense style 4 was higher for the
nonpatients (28.2 v 24.4).

This difference between the nonpatient and the patient sample
in the use of defense styles is again borne out if one examines the
defense styles used by individual subjects. If a subject's score was
0.5 SD above the mean on a particular factor, we considered that
that subject used that corresponding defense style. A cutting point
of 0.5 SD provided the best discrimination here. Of those with
computable scores, 60 percent of the patients used defense style 1

in conjunction with other styles and 16 percent used it exclusively. In contrast, 11 percent of the nonpatients used style 1 in conjunction with other styles and only three percent used it exclusively. With regard to defense style 4, 48 percent of the patients used it in conjunction with other defense styles and only nine percent used it exclusively. In contrast, 90 percent of the nonpatients used defense style 4 in conjunction with other defenses and 42 percent used it exclusively.

The following clinical example illustrates how scores on our scales might relate to clinical information. The patient had a diagnosis of an acute schizophrenic episode and borderline personality at different times. At the time that she was tested, she was an outpatient. At her worst, she showed signs of regression, withdrawal, and primitive projection. She had delusions of persecutions, influence, and grandiosity; however, by structuring her life and by encouraging her activity in the creative arts and music, she was helped to cope.

This patient had high scores on defense styles 1, 2, and 4. We believe that style 1 reflected her regressive behavior, style 2 reflected her omnipotence and primitive idealization, and style 4 reflected her adaptive coping mechanisms. The fact that a subject used multiple styles might provide clues as to why he or she would receive different diagnoses at different times. According to the *DSM-III*, a diagnosis of schizophrenia rules out the diagnosis of borderline personality disorder, but if this patient was using styles 2 and 4 most strongly and her regressive behavior was under control, then she would seem borderline to some clinicians.

COMMENT

Questionnaire

A questionnaire has some important advantages over the clinical interview for the assessment of defensive functioning. It saves time; it does not require highly trained and highly paid professionals to administer it; it eliminates problems of interrater reliability; it can provide a measure of the degree to which defenses are present on a standardizable continuum; and it provides an opportunity to gather normative data. As a result, it permits the development of cutting points that may discriminate between impaired and unimpaired functioning.

Our results demonstrate that the construction of such a questionnaire is feasible. We have produced an instrument that has desirable statistical properties. Even more important, the factors make clinical sense. We do not presume, however, that the present questionnaire is complete. It does not measure all the possible conscious derivatives of defense mechanisms. Nonetheless, it does provide a frame to which questions measuring other defenses or more items measuring the same defenses can be added. It must be stressed, however, that we are only measuring self-appraisals of defensive styles and not actually measuring defense mechanisms. A further study is needed to validate the relationship between what we are measuring and the traditional notion of defense.

A number of findings lend support to the validity of the questionnaire. The internal consistency of the questionnaire was demonstrated by two experimental findings. First, the item-total correlations on the questions and the defenses that they were supposed to represent were all significant ($p < .001$). Second, the defenses clustered in the factor analysis along lines that make theoretical sense. Thus "immature" defense maneuvers (e.g., regression, acting out) clustered together on factor 1; it is possible to think of the defenses of factors 2 and 3 (e.g., splitting, primitive idealization, pseudoaltruism) as intermediate in nature; and the defenses clustered in factor 4 (sublimation, suppression, and humor) are commonly associated with the idea of maturity. Further, the highly negative correlation of the expected primitive defenses with the expected higher level defenses provides additional evidence for internal consistency.

The criterion validity of the questionnaire was supported in two ways. First, the defense styles related to other indices of ego development, as expected—that is, the relative correlations of styles 1 through 4 with the scores on the Loevinger and ego strength tests indicate that they can be ranked, in that order, on a continuum of development or adaptation. Second, the fact that patients tend to use the less mature defenses and nonpatients the higher level defenses adds credence to the questionnaire. The patient sample had significantly higher mean scores than the nonpatient sample on style 1 through 3 defenses. The nonpatient sample had a significantly higher mean score on style 4 defenses. When factor scores were computed for individual subjects, the patients tended to use style 1 defenses much more and the style 4 defenses much less than the nonpatients.

Clusters of Self-Perceptions of Characteristic Defenses

It was clear from our data that subjects' perceptions of their own characteristic behaviors clustered into what we call defensive styles. It is interesting to speculate, for each style, about what the common elements might be that applies to all the inferred defenses associated with that style. For the six defenses that clustered on factor 1—withdrawal, acting out, regression, inhibition, passive aggression, and projection—immaturity may not be the best term since these defenses can sometimes be found in well-functioning persons. Perhaps the common feature of this factor is that all these behaviors indicate the subjects' inability to deal with their impulses by taking constructive action on their own behalf. The acting-out subject requires controls. The withdrawn or inhibited person needs to be actively drawn out. The passive-aggressive person acts to provoke anger in the person with whom he or she is involved. The regressed person requires someone to take over and do something for him. The projecting person puts the blame and responsibility on others instead of accepting his or her own impulses. Thus, this style might be labeled "maladaptive action patterns."

The essence of the inferred defenses that clustered on factor 2—splitting, primitive idealization, and omnipotence with devaluation—is the splitting of the image of self and other into good and bad, strong and weak. This clearly differs from the style 1 defenses in that it is image oriented rather than action oriented. Although style 2 could interfere with object relations, it need not necessarily affect achievement and accomplishment. These defenses could be invoked in the service of constructive adaptation in situations of stress by persons who do not use them habitually—for example, one way of dealing with a severe physical illness may be to trust in the omnipotence of the physician. These defenses may also be used nonadaptively by persons with chronic difficulty in forming mature relationships. In the literature, this style is associated with narcissistic and borderline personality disorders (6). These clustered defenses, then, can be described as the "image-distorting" style.

The items designed to test the two inferred defenses constituting style 3—reaction formation and pseudoaltriusm—reflect a need to perceive one's self as being kind, helpful to others, and never angry. This is characteristic of martyr types and "do-gooders." It is our impression that these people are often involved in stable but not necessarily healthy (often masochistic) relationships and that they are usually able to function adequately. They often come to the attention of psychiatrists when they suffer a loss and their characteristic defense pattern cannot contain their anger and anxiety. They then become depressed. Style 3 can be characterized as consisting of "self-sacrificing" defenses. (We suspect that with a larger sample or with a great number of questions more defenses could have been grouped on this factor. It could evolve into an obsessive-compulsive factor with the addition of intellectualization and the related defenses of undoing and isolation.)

The inferred defenses for style 4—humor, suppression, and sublimation—are clearly associated with good coping. Suppression allows an anxiety-producing conflict to be put out of awareness until one is ready to deal with the issue. Humor reflects a capacity to accept a conflictual situation while taking the edge off its painful aspects. Sublimation uses the anxiety-provoking impulse in the service of creative response. All three defenses are associated with a constructive type of mastery of the conflict. Style 4 can be labeled the "adaptive" defense style.

For the most part, the defense styles are different from the "neurotic styles" Shapiro (14) outlined by means of theoretical construction from psychoanalytic descriptions rather than by using empirical data. He described the obsessive, paranoid, hysterical, and impulsive styles. Our maladaptive action patterns probably correspond to his impulsive style, but the other "neurotic styles" seem to be organized along factors different from our defense styles. It is interesting to compare these different results obtained from different methods, but it is also possible that Shapiro had a different population in mind when constructing his styles.

Maturity and Defense Styles

The correlations of each of the defense styles with two measures of maturity—that is, ego strength and Loevinger tests—indicate that in developmental terms there is a progression from the maladaptive action patterns, through the image-distorting defenses, and the self-sacrificing defenses to the adaptative defenses, along the line of increasingly constructive dealing with the vicissitudes of life.

The least mature people have behavior problems. Those in the image-distorting group have problems in realistically viewing themselves and others, which lends to relationship problems. The self-sacrificing persons have more stable relationships but cannot fulfill their creative potential. The adaptive defenses reflect less preoccupation with relationships and allow more creative expression of one's inner self. Thus, the defensive styles reflect a shift from preoccupation with control of raw impulses, to preoccupation with all-important others, to creative expression of one's self.

Other studies also reflect this shift. With a clinical population, Semrad et al. (9) suggested that as patients improve, their defenses become less primitive and more mature. One patient in their study moved from what they labeled as narcissistic patterns, to affective defensive patterns, to neurotic defensive patterns as therapy progressed. Vaillant (7, 12), in his 20-year follow-up study of a normal male college-age population, found an increasing use of more mature defenses over time. Mature defenses not only enhanced the men's ability to work but also enhanced their ability to love. Thus, Vaillant's study of normal subjects, the study of patients by Semrad et al., and our study of both patients and nonpatients indicate that defenses can be arranged in a hierarchy of maturity that relates to a person's successful adaptation to the world.

FOLLOW-UP ON THE RELATIONSHIP BETWEEN DIAGNOSIS AND DEFENSE STYLE

Methodology

In order to determine how the scores on the defense style questionnaire relate to diagnosis, it was necessary to use a uniform, valid, and reliable diagnostic classification. Diagnoses recorded in the patients' charts were inadequate for this purpose because the attending psychiatrists and psychologists did not all use the same diagnostic criteria and because they did not all distinguish between principal and secondary diagnoses. For these reasons, patients were rediagnosed using their charts, which provided data gathered at the time of the original testing as well as data gathered from subsequent contacts. Two independent raters (a staff psychiatrist and a senior psychiatry resident) applied *DSM-III* criteria and rated patients on Axes, I, II, and IV. Both raters were blind to the defensive styles used by the patients. Charts were available for 74 of the patients who had completed the defense style questionnaire. These patients were diagnosed on Axes I and II by both raters, who recorded principal and secondary diagnoses. Axis IV was used by only one rater, in cases ($N = 48$) where there was adequate information about psychosocial stressors. Axes III and V were not used because of a lack of sufficient information in the charts.

Because of small sample size, the Axis I and Axis II diagnoses were grouped as suggested by Treece (26). Axis I diagnoses were grouped into the following four categories: psychotic disorders (including schizophrenia, paranoia, and schizoaffective disorder), major affective disorders (bipolar and unipolar), anxiety disorders, and other Axis I disorders (including adjustment disorder and dysthymic disorder). Axis II diagnoses were grouped into the following four categories: type A (schizoid, schizotypal, paranoid), type B (histrionic, narcissistic, antisocial, borderline), type C (avoidant, dependent, compulsive, passive-aggressive), and other personality disorders. Raters compared principal diagnoses and reached agreement in 93.2 percent of cases ($N = 69$). Cases where there was disagreement ($N = 5$) were excluded from the analysis. Interrater reliability, calculated by kappa coefficient (27) was .98. This result is higher than literature reports on interrater reliability using Axis I (.78) and Axis II (.61 or less) (28, 29), probably because our data came from charts instead of clinical interviews and because we used broader categories of diagnoses designed to increase the number of cases on which we agreed. It is unlikely that the limitations of case record data (problems with missing data, conflicting descriptions, and differing evaluations of the degree to which a particular behavior is pathological) would affect the value of statistical analysis (30).

Relations between defensive styles and Axes I and II were analyzed in this reduced sample of 69 patients, which did not differ from the original total patient sample ($N = 98$) in terms of age, sex, patient status, chart diagnosis, and defensive styles.

Follow-up Results: Defense Styles and Axes I and II Diagnoses

The original patient group had already been compared to the control group for the number and the types of defense styles used as described previously. Then, each of the different diagnostic categories was compared to the reduced patient sample in terms of the number and the types of defense styles used.

The majority of our 69 patients were in one of the following three diagnostic categories: psychotic disorders ($N = 22$), affective disorders ($N = 16$), and personality disorders type B ($N = 20$). Hence, for calculation purposes, we paired anxiety disorders ($N = 2$) with other Axis I disorders ($N = 5$), and personality disorders type A ($N = 2$) with personality disorders type C ($N = 2$). Calculations were done using the chi-square statistic.

Within the patient group, the most striking finding was that except for affective disorders, no diagnosis was associated with the reported use of any particular number or type of defense style. For patients with affective disorders, the questionnaire responses resulted in a description of "no defense style" more often (44 percent) than in other patients, such as psychotics (five percent) and personality disorders type B (20 percent). Patients with affective disorders reported multiple styles (25 percent) less often than other patients ($\chi^2 = 29.4$, $df = 2$, $p < .001$). Patients with affective disorders reported using the "adaptive" defense style 4 (31 percent) more often than style 1 (19 percent), style 2 (13 percent), and style 3 (25 percent). This pattern of styles was significantly different from that of other patients, who for the most part reported using styles 1, 2, and 3 as often as or more frequently than style 4 ($\chi^2 = 28.1$, $df = 4$, $p < .001$).

DISCUSSION

Although styles 1, 2, and 3 are associated with patient status, defense style could not predict diagnostic category nor could Axis

Table 4. Percentage of Subjects Within Diagnostic Categories (DSM-III Axes I and II) Reporting Using Each Defense Style*

Principal Diagnosis	Percent (number) of Subjects				
	No Style	Style 1	Style 2	Style 3	Style 4
Psychotic disorders ($N = 22$)	5 (1)	36 (8)	36 (8)	41 (9)	36 (8)
Affective disorders ($N = 16$)	44 (7)	19 (3)	13 (2)	25 (4)	31 (5)
Anxiety and other Axis I disorders ($N = 7$)	0 (0)	29 (2)	29 (2)	14 (1)	43 (3)
Personality disorders type B ($N = 20$)	20 (4)	40 (8)	45 (9)	30 (6)	30 (6)
Personality disorders types A and C ($N = 4$)	0 (0)	75 (3)	50 (2)	50 (2)	25 (1)
Total patient group ($N = 69$)	17 (12)	35 (24)	33 (23)	32 (22)	33 (23)
Total control group ($N = 111$)	42 (47)	6 (7)	16 (18)	16 (18)	37 (41)

*Because many subjects reported using multiple defense styles, the sum of percentages in any row may exceed 100.

I, II, or IV diagnoses accurately predict defense style. Most of the patients with major affective disorders used either no style that could be detected or style 4, a combination that resembled the defense pattern of controls more than that of patients. I will offer several possible explanations for this later in this section. However, a minority of patients with affective disorders reported defense patterns typical of other patients, using styles 1, 2, and 3. Our results suggest that diagnosis and defense style may be two independent dimensions. Diagnosis is related to symptoms and pathological behavior, but defense style is related to the way in which one deals with a given situation, whether consciously or unconsciously.

The data reflect the complexity of human psychology and the wide range of human potential. Chodoff and Lyons (31) showed that conversion reactions occur in many personality types, not only and not even more frequently in histrionic personalities. This is consistent with the notion that Axis II cannot predict Axis I and vice versa. Such findings challenge the linear thinking which implies that certain symptoms are a direct outgrowth of a certain personality structure.

Several limitations to our study have to be resolved before our conclusions can be accepted without question. First, we did not measure defense mechanisms directly. Cross-validation with clinicians' ratings of defense mechanisms would be necessary to prove that our factors *actually* represent clusters of defenses. This is a project we are now organizing. As of now, our questionnaire has only construct and face validity.

Second, we may not have enough questions to tap all the defenses that our subjects used. An insufficient number of appropriate statements on the questionnaire or a poorly chosen cutting point may yield too many false negatives (32). In cases where no consistent style was detected, it is possible that the defense or coping mechanisms that these people used were not reflected in the items on the questionnaire. We certainly made no effort to tap the more adaptive processes—for example, self-assertion, self-observation, anticipatory problem-solving—that might be common among nonpatients.

A related point is that some people may not be aware of their defenses as coping mechanisms and thus may not acknowledge them in their responses to the questionnaire. It may be that this type of person is overrepresented among people who have not sought psychiatric help or among those with major affective disorders. At this point we have no way of proving or disproving this.

Third, because we examined broad diagnostic categories rather than specific diagnoses, we might have overlooked significant relationships, particularly between defenses and the Axis II diagnoses. For example, one might expect an obsessive-compulsive personality to use isolation, doing and undoing, reaction formation, and intellectualization. In our factor analysis, only reaction formation loaded strongly on one of the four factors—factor 3, together with pseudoaltruism. Thus, we did not find a clear-cut obsessive-compulsive defense style.

Our sample might have similarly limited our findings. For example, we had only one patient with obsessive-compulsive personality disorder and two with obsessive traits. The former was rated as having no clear defense style and of the latter, one manifested style 3 and the other style 4. If we changed the sample to include a larger number of obsessive-compulsive personalities, the factors yielded by analysis would very likely change, as Meehl and Rosen point out (32). Therefore, we cannot say that we have definitively shown that specific personality disorders do not reliably predict given defense styles.

Another limitation is related to the fact that the patients were tested at only one phase of their illness. Although all outpatients were tested at the time of their intake interview, inpatients might have been very decompensated or on the road to recovery when tested. Although we do not have test-retest data from the same time frame, we do plan to do an eight-year follow-up to shed some light on the state or trait issue.

Even with these limitations, the difference in patients with affective disorders and their resemblance to the control group in their responses to the questionnaire is interesting. This group of patients and the nonpatients rate themselves as either using defenses that are toward the adaptive end of the hierarchy or behaving in a way that was not tapped by the questionnaire.

It is possible that the defense or coping styles that nonpatients use are different from those used by patients with affective disorders and that both are not measured by the questionnaire. It is also possible that these people are different on the basis of a dimension other than defense style—for example, psychodynamic conflicts (33). A third possibility is that patients with affective disorder do have defense styles similar to those of nonpatients and that their decompensation into patienthood is related to a biochemical factor rather than the defense style.

Our main finding in the follow-up study is that there was not a clear relationship between defense style as measured by the questionnaire and *DSM-III* diagnosis. However, this finding does not mean that we have proved that defense style and diagnosis are independent dimensions. Our data are consistent, though, with the notion that people with the same diagnosis can use many different defense styles. This echoes the views of Karasu (34) and Strayhorn (35), who advocate a sixth axis for *DSM-III* in order to offer more discriminating information about the psychodynamics or resources of patients with the same Axis I or II diagnosis. Along this line, Clarkin et al. point out the heterogeneity within the diagnostic category of borderline personality disorder and find prototypic typology to be responsible (36). Defense styles constitute one way of describing those heterogeneous features.

When used in conjunction with clinical data, information about patients' defense styles can help the clinician to plan the subtleties of treatment. The form that a sixth axis should take is properly the task of a work group to revise the *DSM-III*, but our data suggest that defense mechanisms or styles certainly would not be a redundant addition to the diagnostic schema.

Our questionnaire has been used in research at other centers, and the same styles emerged after factor analysis, consistent with theoretical expectations. Thus indirect evidence of validity is accumulating. However, our current research is designed to take a further leap toward validity.

We intend to have Christopher Perry train our raters, using the manual for the Defense Mechanism Clinical Rating Scale developed by Perry and Cooper (part IV of the Appendix). Our raters will then rate videotaped assessment interviews of patients coming for psychiatric evaluations in our department. These subjects will also complete our self-report questionnaire. A comparison of these scores will determine whether the two techniques are measuring the same phenomena. Of course, many pitfalls will still remain and many questions will still have to be answered. Of necessity this is the natural course for the study of inferred intrapsychic processes. We hope that the attempt to measure these elusive defense mechanisms empirically will shed light on the limits of what researchers and clinicians can and cannot claim to know about them and their relationships to other aspects of human functioning.

References

1. Bond M, Gardner ST, Christian J, et al: Empirical study of self-rated defense styles. Arch Gen Psychiatry 40:333-338, 1983

2. Bond M, Sagala Vaillant J: Empirical study of the relationship between diagnosis and defense style: Arch Gen Psychiatry (in press)

3. Laplanche J, Pontalis JB: The Language of Psychoanalysis. London, Hogarth Press, 1973

4. Freud S: Inhibitions, symptoms and anxiety (1926), in The Complete Psychological Works, vol. 20. Translated by Strachy J. London, Hogarth Press, 1973

5. Freud A: The Ego and the Mechanisms of Defense (1937). New York, International Universities Press, 1966

6. Kernberg O: Borderline personality organization. J Am Psychoanal Assoc 15:641-685, 1967

7. Vaillant GE: Natural history of male psychological health, V: the relation of choice of ego mechanisms of defense to adult adjustment. Arch Gen Psychiatry 33:535-545, 1976

8. Haan NA, Stroud J, Holstein J: Moral and ego stages in relationship to ego processes: a study of "hippies." J Pers 41:596-612, 1973

9. Semrad EV, Grinspoon L, Feinberg SE: Development of an ego profile scale. Arch Gen Psychiatry 28:70-77, 1973

10. Klein M: The Psychoanalysis of Children. London, Hogarth Press, 1973

11. Bellak L, Hurvich M, Gediman HK: Ego Functions in Schizophrenics, Neurotics, and Normals. New York, John Wiley & Sons, 1973

12. Vaillant GE: Natural history of male psychological health, III: empirical dimensions of mental health. Arch Gen Psychiatry 32:420-426, 1975

13. Haan NA: Triparite model of ego functioning values and clinical research applications. J Nerv Ment Dis 148:14-30, 1969

14. Shapiro D: Neurotic Styles. New York, Basic Books, 1965

15. Loevinger J: Ego Development. San Francisco, Jossey-Bass, 1976

16. Loevinger J, Wessler R: Measuring Ego Development. Vol 1: Construction and Use of a Sentence Completion Test. San Francisco, Jossey-Bass, 1970

17. Aronoff J: A Test and Scoring Manual for the Measurement of Safety, Love and Belongingness, and Esteem Needs. East Lansing, MI, Department of Psychology, Michigan State University, 1971

18. Blasi A, cited by Loevinger J, Wessler R: Measuring Ego Development. Vol 1: Construction and Use of a Sentence Completion Test. San Francisco, Jossey-Bass, 1970

19. Hauser ST: Loevinger's model and measure of ego development: a critical review. Psychol Bull 83:928-955, 1976

20. Cox N: Prior help, ego development, and helping behavior. Child Dev 45:594-603, 1974

21. Blasi A: A Developmental Approach to Responsibility Training. St. Louis, Ph.D. dissertation. Washington University, 1972

22. Hoppe C: Ego Development and Conformity Behavior. St. Louis, Ph.D. dissertation. Washington University, 1972

23. Loevinger J: The meaning and measurement of ego development. Am Psychol 21:195-206, 1966

24. Frank S, Quinlan D, quoted by Hauser ST: Loevinger's model and measurement of ego development: a critical review. Psychol Bull 83: 928-955, 1976

25. Nie NH, Hull CH, Jenkins JG, et al: Statistical Package for the Social Sciences, second edition. New York, McGraw-Hill, 1975

26. Treece C: *DSM-III* as a research tool. Am J Psychiatry 139:577-583, 1982

27. Spitzer RL, Cohen J, Fleiss J, et al: Quantification of agreement in psychiatric diagnosis: a new approach. Arch Gen Psychiatry 17:83-87, 1967

28. Spitzer RL, Forman JBW, Nee J: *DSM-III* field trials, I: initial interrater diagnostic reliability. Am J Psychiatry 136:815-817, 1979

29. Mellsop G, Varghese F, Joshua S, et al: The reliability of Axis II of *DSM-III*. Am J Psychiatry 139:1360-1361, 1982

30. Straus JS, Harder DW: The Case Record Rating Scale: a method for rating symptom and social function data from case records. Psychiatry Res 4:333-345, 1981

31. Chodoff P, Lyons H: Hysteria, the hysterical personality and "hysterical conversion." Am J Psychiatry 114:734-740, 1958

32. Meehl PE, Rosen A: Antecedent probability and the efficiency of psychometric signs, patterns or cutting scores. Psychol Bull 52:194-215, 1955

33. Perry JC, Cooper SH: A preliminary report on defenses and conflicts associated with borderline personality disorder. J Am Psychoanal Assoc (in press)

34. Karasu T, Skodol A: Sixth axis for *DSM-III*: psychodynamic evaluation. Am J Psychiatry 137:607-610, 1980

35. Strayhorn G: A diagnostic axis relevant to psychotherapy and preventive mental health. Am J Orthopsychiatry 53:677-696, 1983

36. Clarkin JF, Widiger, TA, Frances A, et al: Prototypic typology and the borderline pesonality disorder. J Abnorm Psychol 92:263-275, 1983

2

What Do Cross-Sectional Measures of Defense Mechanisms Predict?

J. Christopher Perry, M.D., M.P.H.
Steven H. Cooper, Ph.D.

2

What Do Cross-Sectional Measures of Defense Mechanisms Predict?

Defense mechanisms and intrapsychic conflict are two concepts that have remained at the core of psychodynamic approaches to clinical psychopathology. As indicated by previous chapters, Freud's initial definition, in 1894, of the defense of projection was eventually followed by descriptions of numerous specific defense mechanisms by psychodynamic clinicians. A defense is a mechanism that mediates between the individual's wishes, needs, affects, and impulses on the one hand and both internalized prohibitions and external reality on the other. Defenses are considered mechanisms only in the sense that they function without conscious effort, and they often follow lawful patterns wherein individuals may repeatedly employ the same defenses.

While the clinician may find a patient's defense mechanisms meaningful to identify and work with, researchers have been slow to study them. For one, as Vaillant comments in his introduction, different authors, such as Anna Freud (1), Fenichel (2), Kernberg (3), Vaillant (4, 5), and Meissner (6), have selected and defined the defenses differently. Vaillant (5) has noted that there is as yet no basis for a definitive list of defense mechanisms and their defini-

This work was supported in part by a grant from the National Institute of Mental Health RO1 MH-34123.

tions that could be made into a psychodynamic "periodic table," as in the physical sciences. A second complication arises because definitions of defenses do not generally specify the rules of inference to determine whether an individual uses a particular defense. Instead, this is left to clinical judgment, which makes it difficult to carry out reliable research on defense mechanisms. Third, a problem arises in specifying the proper data source for observing defenses. Is it the psychodynamic interview, the therapist's summaries of treatment, a questionnaire, or the individual's response to life stress? Each of these data sources yields observations with different clinical implications. Even when measurement questions are adequately addresssed, a fourth problem remains, for little is known about the validity of the defense constructs. What, for instance, do they predict about human functioning?

This chapter reports on a study of personality and affective disorders that has employed both cross-sectional and longitudinal measures of defensive functioning. The study addresses the following questions:

1. Can defenses be reliabily measured, first, from observing videotaped psychodynamic interviews, and second, from rating reports of an individual's response to life events?

2. What is the relationship between defense mechanisms measured at intake and prospectively observed clinical symptoms?

3. What do defense mechanisms predict about future psychosocial functioning?

4. Do defenses observed in the interview situation predict defensive functioning in response to life stressors?

METHODS

Sample

The subjects for the present study are drawn from an ongoing study of personality and affective disorders (7, 8). Subjects were selected for having borderline personality disorder or borderline traits, antisocial personality disorder, or bipolar type II. They were initially interviewed and diagnosed by the authors. All BPD subjects met *DSM-III* criteria and scored about 150 on the Borderline Personality Scale, second version (BPS-II), which is an earlier version of the Borderline Personality Disorder Scale (BPD Scale). Subjects with borderline traits met four *DSM-III* criteria and fell within a lower cutoff score on the BPS-II, but did not meet criteria for BPD. ASP was diagnosed according to *DSM-III*, and bipolar type II according to the Research Diagnostic Criteria (9).

Subsequent data analyses used two continuous personality measures to increase diagnostic sensitivity: the 36-item BPD Scale for borderline psychopathology, and the ASP Score, a count of the positive symptoms from *DSM-III* weighted to favor symptoms present in the past five years, to measure antisociality.

Instrument Construction

The Clinical Defense Mechanism Rating Scales (CDMRS) consist of 22 defense mechanisms representing immature (5), borderline (3), and neurotic (5, 6) levels of defensive functioning. We initially selected those defenses most relevant to the study of personality pathology, omitting both psychotic and mature defenses. The rating manual contains a formal definition of each defense, an explanation of its function, and a discussion of how to discriminate it from other defenses. (See part IV, Appendix, for description of CDMRS and a glossary of the 22 definitions. In addition, definitions are included for eight mature defenses not reported on here.) Each defense is rated on a three-point scale as not present, probably present, or definitely present. Each scale point is anchored with examples. (See the example of neurotic denial in part IV, Appendix.) The scales can be applied to psychodynamically oriented interview data, such as might be obtained in an initial psychotherapy interview.

Procedures

Subjects had a psychodynamically oriented interview with an experienced clinician, usually within six weeks of joining the study. A videotape of the interview served as the data base from which ratings were made. Six research assistants served as raters; half of them were in graduate school, and only one had no previous clinical experience. Raters were divided into two groups of three each. After each group of three observed a videotape, the individuals rated the subject for the 22 defenses. They then discussed each defense and reached a group consensus for the ratings. The consensus ratings were used for subsequent analyses.

Reliability was assessed in two subsamples. The first group consisted of 22 subjects with personality disorders or bipolar type II; the second group consisted of 24 subjects, eight with personality disorders, eight with bipolar II, and eight with neurotic character problems—reflecting a mix more representative of an outpatient clinic population. The eight neurotic patients were used in the reliability sample only. Because the samples yielded similar medians and ranges of reliability coefficients, they were combined ($n = 46$) to yield more stable reliability estimates, which are reported below.

In order to facilitate data analysis, we decided to pare down the number of defenses by combining some of them. We grouped conceptually related defenses that were empirically intercorrelated into five summary defense scales, described below. Separate reliability figures were then calculated for these:

Projection, neurotic denial, bland denial, and rationalization were combined into a *disavowal* summary scale because they all disavow experiences.

Acting out, passive aggression, and hypochondriasis were combined into the *action* summary scale because each defense releases feelings and impulses through action.

Splitting of self and others' images and projective identification were combined into a *borderline* summary defense scale.

Omnipotence, primitive idealization, and devaluation were combined into a *narcissistic* summary scale because each serves to regulate self-esteem and mood.

Isolation, intellectualization, and undoing, which neutralize affects, were combined into an *obsessional* scale.

The low intercorrelation of repression and other defenses did not support the construction of a hysterical defenses scale, so that the only neurotic-level summary scale is the obsessional one. A factor analysis reported elsewhere (10) supported the separation of borderline from narcissistic defenses.

Follow-up Measures

After entry into the study, subjects were interviewed every three months for three years. Research assistants gathered information for month-by-month ratings on each of the following areas:

1. Four types of symptoms were rated over the first one to two years of the follow-up period using the Hamilton Rating Scale (HRS) for depression (11), and three Psychiatric Status Schedule (PSS) measures for drug, alcohol, and antisocial symptoms (12). The subject's median value for each scale was used as a summary of his or her general level of that symptom for the whole follow-up period.
2. Seven areas of psychosocial functioning were rated on six-point scales beginning the second or third year of follow-up. The proportion of months in which the subject was rated as moderately impaired or worse was calculated and expressed as the likelihood (odds) of being impaired for the whole follow-up period. To normalize these outcome variables, the log of the odds (or logit) was used in analyses.
3. Global functioning was rated on the Global Assessment Scale (GAS) (13), and the subject's median score over the follow-up period was used.

Because some of the psychosocial variables were highly intercorrelated, for some analyses they were combined into two factors derived by factor analysis. The first factor combined impairment in roles relating to occupation, relatives, and overall satisfaction with life. The second factor combined impairment with lover or spouse, friends, general socializing, and leisure. These two factors (in reverse order) correspond roughly to the capacities for "leiben und arbeiten" (love and work), which Freud gave as his description of health. The follow-up interviews also focused on life events that occurred in the subjects' lives over the previous three-month interval. Information on each event was collected in a semi-structured format resembling the method used by George Brown (14) in the Camberwell depression study. The information gathered concerned the stressors, the subjects' role in bringing them about, and what their responses were to each event. Such collective information is known as a life vignette and served as the data base for rating subjects' prospective use of defenses.

Ratings were made as follows. A pair of raters read each life vignette for a given subject's three-month follow-up and made independent ratings of up to five defenses per vignette, using the same manual as in the videotaped interview method. After discussing their individual ratings, the raters agreed on consensus ratings, which were used for subsequent analyses. The subjects' defense scores were calculated as the proportion (0 to 1.0) of life vignettes within each follow-up period in which a given defense was used. When several follow-ups were available, the average score for each defense was used in data analyses.

Of 91 subjects who entered the study, 72 were videotaped and rated for defenses. Of these, 55 had at least one follow-up available for rating prospective psychosocial functioning. At present only 24 subjects have been rated for defensive functioning on at least one follow-up.

RESULTS

Our first question, as set forth early in this chapter, addressed the reliability of the two methods for rating defense mechanisms. For the videotaped interview method, the intraclass coefficient was calculated for each of the 22 individual defenses. For individual raters ($n = 46$, raters = 6), the median reliability was .36 with a range of .11 to .59. These values were higher for the consensus ratings ($n = 46$, consensus groups = 2), for which the median reliability figure was .57 with a range of .35 to .79. For the life

Table 1. Defenses' Prediction of Symptoms Over One- to Two-Year
Follow-up: Spearman Correlations ($N = 67$)

Follow-up: Symptom Measures Administered at Three-Month Intervals; Range Two to
Seven Administrations
Subjects' Median Score Over Follow-Up[a]

	HRS Depression	PSS Drugs	PSS Alcohol	PSS Antisocial
Summary Defense				
Disavowal	.25*	.17	.32**	.33**
Action	.51**	.33**	.25*	.30**
Borderline	.20*	.16	−.03	.06
Narcissistic	.07	.18	.14	.25*
Obsessional	−.32**	.10	−.03	.07

[a] HRS = Hamilton Rating Scale (11); PSS = Psychiatric Status Schedule (12).
*$p = .05$; **$p = .01$.

vignette method ($n = 24$, raters = 2), the median value of the individual ratings of 13 of the defenses was .64 with a range from .38 to 1.0. Given the small sample, the remaining defenses were rated fewer than four times on the vignettes, and therefore reliability was not calculated.

The reliability of the five summary defense scales is generally at acceptable levels for both the interview and the life vignette methods. The median value of the consensus ratings ($n = 46$, consensus groups = 2) for the videotaped interview method was .74 with a range of .57 to .78, while for the life vignette method the median value was .64 with a range of .45 to .80 for the individual raters. These reliability figures are as high as those obtained for most of the personality disorders on Axis II.

The remainder of the analyses focused on possible answers to our other three questions, which were concerned with what observed defenses could predict about patient symptoms and functioning. Table 1, responding to the second question, demonstrates the relationship between the summary defense scales rated at entry and subsequent levels of clinical symptoms over the first one to two years of follow-up. The action defenses predicted—that is, were correlated with—higher levels of drug, alcohol, and antisocial symptoms and were very highly predictive of depressive symptoms. The disavowal defenses predicted both alcohol and antisocial symptoms, and, to a lesser extent, depressive symptoms. Borderline defenses predicted depressive symptoms only, while narcissistic defenses predicted antisocial symptoms. Finally, obsessional defenses predicted lower levels of depressive symptoms in this sample. Overall, the defense summary scales were moderately predictive of the general levels of these four types of symptoms over the first year or two of the follow-up period.

Table 2. Defenses' Prediction of Longitudinal Psychosocial Functioning: Spearman Correlations (N = 55)

	Median GAS[a]	Impairment Factors	
		I	II
		Work, Relatives, Satisfaction	Lover, Friend, Social, Leisure
	− = worse	+ = worse	+ = worse
1. Immature Defenses			
Neurotic denial	−.15	.15	.20
Projection	−.29*	.29*	.27*
Hypochondriasis	−.46***	.27*	.40**
Passive–aggression	−.40**	.35**	.32*
Acting out	−.29*	.18	.26*
Fantasy	−.02	.02	.31*
2. Borderline Defenses			
Splitting of self images	−.27*	.29*	.10
Splitting of others' images	−.35**	.33**	.29*
Manic–depressive denial	−.14	.09	.11
Bland denial	−.29*	.33**	.24
Projective identification	−.13	.11	.09
Primitive idealization	.05	.02	−.11
Omnipotence	.05	−.08	.07
Devaluation	−.28*	.21	.27*
3. Neurotic Defenses			
Repression	.11	−.02	.05
Dissociation	−.01	.15	.07
Displacement	−.17	.32*	.08
Reaction formation	.03	.20	−.23
Isolation	.25	−.32*	−.14
Intellectualization	.38**	−.48***	−.34**
Rationalization	.00	.00	.04
Undoing	.20	−.14	−.07

[a]GAS = Global Assessment Scale (13).
*p = .05; **p = .01; ***p = .001.

Table 3. Summary Defenses' Prediction of Longitudinal Psychosocial
Functioning: Spearman Correlations (N = 55)

	Median GAS[a]	Impairment Factors	
		I	II
		Work, Relatives, Satisfaction	Lover Friends, Social, Leisure
	− = worse	+ = worse	+ = worse
Summary Defense Scales			
Disavowal	−.26*	.27*	.28*
Action	−.53***	.35**	.44***
Borderline	−.27*	.29*	.20
Narcissistic	−.07	.05	.09
Obsessional	.35**	−.44***	−.27*

[a]GAS = Global Assessment Scale (13).
*p = .05; **p = .01; ***p = .001.

Table 2 is concerned with the third question, what do defense
mechanisms predict about future psychosocial functioning? The
individual immature defenses generally bode ill for psychosocial
functioning two to three years later. Projection, hypochondriasis,
passive aggression, and, to a lesser extent, acting out all predicted
lower average global functioning in our subjects, and a higher
proportion of follow-ups with impairment in both work and love
areas. Schizoid fantasy, on the other hand, did not predict global
functioning or impairment with work but did predict impairment
in love and social areas.

The eight borderline level defenses, as defined by Kernberg (3),
also tended to predict negative outcomes. Splitting of self and
others' images and bland denial predicted lower GAS and higher
impairment with work, relatives, and satisfaction. In addition,
splitting of others' images also predicted impairment with love
and other relations. Of the three defenses at this level that we call
narcissistic, only devaluation predicted significant negative functioning.

The neurotic level defenses yielded a different pattern. Most of
them were not correlated significantly with global functioning or

impairment factors. The exceptions are as follows. In this sample, intellectualization was associated with higher global functioning and a lower proportion of impairment in all social roles. Isolation also predicted significantly less impairment on the factor of work, relatives, and satisfaction. In contrast, individuals with a marked use of the displacement defense had impairment with work, relatives, and satisfaction.

Table 3 addresses the third question in terms of the five summary defense scales, displaying their relationship to global functioning and the two psychosocial impairment factors for the follow-up period. The action defenses are the most powerful predictors of poorer outcome and increased likelihood of impairment. The disavowal and borderline defenses are next in magnitude as predictors of poorer functioning. The narcissistic defenses have negligible predictive power, while the obsessional defenses again predict better functioning and less impairment overall.

Table 4 addresses the final question, whether cross-sectional ratings of defenses predict future defensive functioning in response to actual life stressors. The Table shows the intercorrelations of the summary defense variables as initially rated (from the videotaped interview at intake) with the same defense variables rated from the follow-up life vignettes ($n = 24$). The disavowal, action, and borderline defenses demonstrate significant ability to predict use of the same defenses in the future. The narcissistic

Table 4. Spearman Correlations Between Cross-Sectional (Videotape) and Longitudinal (Life Vignettes) Ratings of Summary Defense Scales ($N = 24$)

	Cross-Sectional Ratings of Defenses at Entry				
	Disavowal	Action	Borderline	Narcissistic	Obsessional
Follow-up Life Vignettes					
Disavowal	.46**	−.01	.28	.15	−.12
Action	.16	.35*	.17	.07	−.39*
Borderline	.13	.25	.38*	−.07	−.55***
Narcissistic	.32	.23	−.01	.26	−.14
Obsessional	−.19	.01	−.22	−.25	−.18

*$p = .10$; **$p = .05$; ***$p = .01$.

defenses show a trend in the same direction. The nonsignificant but negative relationship of the obsessional defenses with themselves is puzzling. This may be a chance finding, since an examination of the life vignette data showed that two of the constituent defenses, isolation and undoing, were never rated in this small sample, thus making a strict comparison of the scales problematic. However, intellectualization did not correlate with itself, which suggests that there may be a problem with the sensitivity of the follow-up method to this defense.

DISCUSSION

This study has examined the reliabiilty and validity of two methods for measuring defense mechanisms. We have found that defense mechanisms can be rated with equal reliability using video-taped psychodynamic interviews, or descriptions of actual life vignettes on follow-up. The reliability of the defenses increases when related defenses are combined into summary defense variables. Defenses rated at admission to the study have predictive validity across three different domains: clinical symptoms, psychosocial functioning, and defensive functioning. These are powerful predictors.

The defenses used by this sample of individuals with personality and affective disorders can be interpreted, therefore, by examining their future effects.

Acting out, passive aggression, and hypochondriasis each allows the individual to direct impulses, feelings, and actions toward others. But rather than solve emotional problems, these defenses ensnarl others through attempts to turn one's own problems into somebody else's problems. They are more likely to seem offensive than defensive to others. They provoke others to try to control rather than to understand their user, and they invite blame, punishment, and ultimately rejection. They are also stable defenses, in the sense that individuals who tend to use them at one time still use them two and three years later. Because these defenses also predict ongoing affective and impulsive symptoms, it is not true, as is popularly thought, that the acting-out individual does not suffer the consequences. The consequences follow him or her through time. Thus, the action defenses presage lower overall functioning and a greater likelihood of impairment in both occupational and interpersonal areas.

Denial, projection, rationalization, and bland denial are defenses that allow the individual to disavow something about himself or herself. However, they hide malfunction better from their user than they do from others. They allow individuals to believe that their emotional problems are minimal, but they do not prevent the consequences of genuine problems. Disavowal defenses predict antisocial, alcohol, and depressive symptoms; lower global functioning; and a likelihood of impairment in work and love relationships. Finally, they predict their own continued use in dealing with subsequent life events. Using defenses to disavow personal emotional problems may give one a temporary holiday from them, but ultimately it seems to compound the emotional consequences.

Splitting of self images, splitting of others' images, and projective identification are defenses that protect one from being aware of conflict over good and bad aspects of the self and others. Rather than bear ambivalent feelings, the individual uses these three borderline defenses temporarily to define all aspects of the self or others as having the same emotional weight. But these defenses leave their users vulnerable. They predict increased depressive symptoms, lower global functioning, and higher impairment in the area of work, relatives, and personal satisfaction. These defenses, too, are stable, so that individuals who use them continue to separate the world artificially into good and bad camps as they deal with subsequent life events.

The narcissistic defenses primarily help the individual deal with problems of self-esteem by overvaluing or devaluing aspects of the self and others. These defenses did predict antisocial symptoms in this sample, but they did not predict global functioning or changes in psychosocial role functioning. There was a trend suggesting that the use of narcissistic defenses was stable throughout the follow-up period. Overall, these defenses were the least predictive of subjects' symptoms or functioning on follow-up. Possibly such defenses regulate subjective self-esteem, but do not affect psychosocial functioning.

In Vaillant's (15) report of the relationship between defenses in young adulthood and later mental health, neurotic defenses (e.g., repression, displacement, intellectualization) did not correlate one way or the other with health. The present findings corroborate this. Partly because these defenses are ubiquitous in this sample, they cannot predict, but the obsessional defenses are an exception. Isolation, intellectualization, and undoing serve to distance their user from feelings but leave awareness of events intact. In a sample of persons with affective and personality disorders, this ability is an advantage. As a result, obsessional defenses predicted lower levels of depression, higher global functioning, and the possibility of improved rather than impaired social functioning. It is unclear whether this relationship to healthier functioning would remain true in a healthier subject sample. A possibly relevant finding is that the life vignettes did not demonstrate that obsessional defenses are stably present, but measurement problems and our small follow-up sample may be responsible for this finding.

CONCLUSION

The increased interest in the biological basis of psychiatric disorders is yielding many valuable findings. Studies such as the present one suggest that equally powerful findings may await those who apply systematic methods to psychodynamic exploration as well. We believe that the relatively new scientific approaches to studying psychodynamics should continue to focus on measurement issues such as the reliability, stability, and predictive validity of psychodynamic constructs. After refinement of measurement procedures, our attention may fruitfully turn to elucidating the relationships between these constructs and behavior. Just as philosophers are continually rethinking the mind-body problem, so should clinician scientists explore both aspects in the field of psychiatry. The study of defense mechanisms is one valid way to work toward this end.

References

1. Freud A: The Ego and the Mechanisms of Defense. New York, International Universities Press, 1966

2. Fenichel O: The Psychoanalytic Theory of Neurosis. New York, W.W. Norton, 1945

3. Kernberg O: Borderline personality organization. J Am Psychoanal Assoc 15:641-685, 1967

4. Vaillant GE: Theoretical hierarchy of adaptive ego mechanisms. Arch Gen Pschiatry 24:107-118, 1971

5. Vaillant GE: Adaptation to Life. Boston, Little, Brown, 1977

6. Meissner WW: Theories of personality and psychopathology: classical psychoanalysis, in Comprehensive Textbook of Psychiatry (Third Edition). Edited by Kaplan HI, Freedman AH, Sadock BJ. Baltimore, Williams and Wilkins, 1980

7. Perry JC: Depression in borderline personality disorder: lifetime prevalence and longitudinal course of symptoms. Am J Psychiatry 142:15-21, 1985

8. Perry JC, Cooper SH: Psychodynamics, symptoms and outcomes in borderline and antisocial personality disorders and bipolar type II affective disorder, in The Borderline: Current Empirical Research. Edited by McGlashan T. Washington DC, American Psychiatric Press, 1985

9. Spitzer RL, Endicott J, Robins E: Research diagnostic criteria: rationale and reliability. Arch Gen Psychiatry 35:773-782, 1978

10. Perry JC, Cooper, SH: A preliminary report on defenses and conflcits associated with borderline personality disorder. J Am Psychoanal Assoc (in press)

11. Hamilton M: A rating scale for depression. J Neurol Neurosurg Psychiatry 23:56-62, 1960

12. Spitzer RL, Endicott J, Fleiss JL, et al: The Psychiatric Status Schedule: a technique for evaluating psychopathology and impairment in role functioning. Arch Gen Psychiatry 23:41-55, 1970

13. Endicott J, Spitzer RL, Fleiss JL, et al: The Global Assessment Scale. Arch Gen Psychiatry 33:766-771, 1976

14. Brown GW, Harris T: The Social Origins of Depression. New York, Free Press, 1978

15. Vaillant GE: Natural history of male psychological health, v: the relation of choice of ego mechanisms of defense to adult adjustment. Arch Gen Psychiatry 33:535-545, 1976

3

An Approach to Evaluating Adolescent Ego Defense Mechanisms Using Clinical Interviews

Alan M. Jacobson, M.D.
William Beardslee, M.D.
Stuart T. Hauser, M.D., Ph.D.
Gil G. Noam, Dipl. Psych.
Sally I. Powers, Ed.D.

3

An Approach to Evaluating Adolescent Ego Defense Mechanisms Using Clinical Interviews

Call me Ishmael. Some years ago . . . I thought I would sail about a little and see the watery part of the world. It is a way I have of driving off the spleen, and regulating the circulation. Whenever I find myself growing grim about the mouth; whenever it is a damp, drizzly November in my soul; whenever I find myself involuntarily pausing before coffin warehouses, and bringing up the rear of every funeral I meet; and especially whenever my hypos get such an upper hand of me, that it requires a strong moral principle to prevent me from deliberately stepping into the street, and methodically knocking people's hats off—then, I account it high time to get to sea as soon as I can. This is my substitute for pistol and ball. (1)

The perspective that underlying issues can motivate thoughts and actions has become part of the fabric of human thought. While the linkages often remain mysterious, the psychiatrist, like the novelist, attempts to bring them forth. Thus, the concept of ego mechanisms of defense is imbedded in psychodynamic reasoning about patients and in the theoretical and clinical literature (2, 3). On the other hand, as previous chapters have pointed out, relatively few investigators have developed empirical methods for their assessment, and definitions of individual defenses often vary

Supported by NIH grants AM 20530 and AM 27845, and grants from the Spencer Foundation, the American Psychoanalytic Research Foundation, and the NIMH.

in their use by clinicians and researchers alike (4–6). As a consequence, the value of these constructs for systematic research, clinical practice, and training is limited. The development of reliable and valid methods for assessing defense mechanisms could prove useful in these endeavors. Recognition of this potential usefulness has, for example, led to consideration of a diagnostic axis for defense and coping mechanisms in the *Diagnostic and Statistical Manual of Mental Disorders, Third Edition (DSM-III)* (7) and its revision *DSM-III-R.*

Because of our research group's interest in assessing developmental processes that are relevant for understanding coping during adolescence, we have constructed a method for objectively evaluating ego defense mechanisms from clinical interview material. The work of constructing a coding procedure has been one facet of a longitudinal study of family contexts of adolescent development. The study has two primary, interrelated aims: 1) to use rigorous empirical methods for examination of specific psychological processes identified by clinical observations as relevant during early and middle adolescence; and 2) to assess the influence of family interaction patterns on adolescent psychosocial development (8). Among the developmental processes we evaluate are adolescent self-images, self-esteem, and ego development (8–10). The assessment of ego defenses provides one other important way to characterize adolescent psychosocial development. These relatively discrete processes may be especially relevant for understanding aspects of adaptation during this complex developmental era.

In this chapter we present our approach to evaluating defense mechanisms and information regarding the reliability of the codes.

ASSESSMENT OF DEFENSE MECHANISMS

Background

Two basic approaches have been taken to assess defense mechanisms: 1) self-report questionnaires; and 2) clinical observer ratings. Self-report questionnaires depend on the conscious description or recognition by the subject of his or her own typical behaviors (3, 4, 11). For example, Bond et al. (4) developed a measure of individual defenses that relies upon the individual's responses to statements designed to tap characteristic styles of dealing with conflictual situations. Subjects report their degree of agreement or disagreement with each statement. This type of approach has the virtue of minimizing problems of interrater reliability, assessment time, and professional participation in the evaluation process. It can be used to derive characteristic and consciously recognized behavior patterns for individuals and groups. Its major disadvantage stems from the data source: a limited number of standardized statements that the subject can evaluate and consciously choose between. Thus, such measures assess conscious derivatives of defenses but may fail to identify particular areas of individual conflict in which defense style may be more critical and in which the subject remains unaware of defense usage. Indeed, from a theoretical perspective, individuals would be expected to remain unaware of defense mechanisms engaged in response to unconscious conflicts. In addition, subjects may select responses in terms of socially or personally desired behaviors. Finally, this type of measure identifies hypothetical rather than actual patterns of defense.

Clinician ratings or judgments of defenses have been utilized by several researchers (5, 6, 12–15). The major values of these approaches include the closeness of the data to the kinds of observations made in clinical practice, the richness of data, and the opportunity to detect unconscious processes present in the behaviors of the patient, which can be observed during interactions with staff and in associations during interviews. Ratings of defenses from directly observed behavior, including clinical interviews, may be particularly useful in studies that evaluate psychotherapeutic outcomes. The limitations of these approaches include difficulty in developing reliable ratings, need for professional input, subject time, and variability in the data base caused by interview style or method of observation.

Within the group of investigators using the clinical rating approach, there has been a variety of differences such as conception of defenses, sources of data, and methods of rating (5, 6, 12–15).

Investigators often hold strikingly different conceptions of the nature of defense mechanisms. For example, Haan views defenses as pathological and as at one end of an adaptation spectrum, with coping at the opposite end (5). On the other hand, Vaillant views defenses as being on a hierarchy from more immature or pathological to more adaptive or mature (6). In addition to defenses, Prelinger and Zimet assessed ego functioning from the perspective of competencies found in styles of thinking and behaving. While they termed this aspect of ego functioning "adaptive strengths," defenses were not viewed as specifically pathological (14). Vaillant (6), Valenstein and his colleagues (15), and Prelinger and Zimet (14) utilize defense ratings that derive from traditional psychoanalytic definitions and conceptualizations.

Sources of data vary widely ranging from interviews (5, 14, 15); interviews plus biographical information (6); to observations in ward settings (12, 13). However variable, the data that form the basis of evaluations consistently derive, at least in part, from direct observations of subjects.

Approaches to coding defenses also vary. Haan uses trained coders to rate defense and coping using a Q-sort method (5). Prelinger used defense and adaptive strength codes with definitions having scaled levels of intensity and examples from interviews that exemplify scale points (14). Vaillant reviews interview material and biographical information to draw vignettes that demonstrate defenses in action. Coders then rate these vignettes in terms of specific defenses.

The complexity involved in developing a systematic, reliable coding system for assessing clinical material has limited the number of investigations that use clinical rating approaches, as well as the construction of a single method that is widely accepted by multiple researchers. In forming our coding method, we have built on these prior efforts to rate ego defenses clinically. In addition to using defense assessments for understanding adolescent development and coping, this work may stimulate the further evolution of a broadly applicable coding method for assessing defense mechanisms from clinical material.

To broaden our perspective on the assessment of coping, we

have also been engaged in constructing an additional coding method for assessing adaptive ego processes, based on a psychoanalytic ego psychological framework (14) and work in the assessment of competence in children, as reported elsewhere (16, 17). While we are using two distinct approaches to evaluation of coping, like Prelinger and Zimet (14) we assume that defenses can serve adaptive functions and do not simply represent a pathological end of the spectrum of individual coping. This conception is quite consistent with that of Vaillant (6) but differs distinctly from that of Haan (5).

Samples Being Studied

To identify a wide range of adolescent developmental patterns, we have followed clinically defined samples of adolescent subjects who are likely to be developmentally impaired or at risk for future impairment, plus a nonpatient sample not at apparent risk for developmental impairment. The three groups of early adolescent subjects followed in this study were recruited between the ages of 12 and 16:

1. Diabetic adolescents were drawn from consecutive registrants at a camp for patients with diabetes or from consecutive admissions to the teaching and treatment unit of the Joslin Diabetes Center. Patients hospitalized in this setting were not acutely ill but had been admitted to refine their understanding or control of their diabetes.

2. Psychiatric patients were drawn from consecutive admissions to the adolescent inpatient unit of a large private teaching hospital. We excluded patients for whom admission evaluation suggested a diagnosis of psychosis or organic brain syndrome.

3. Adolescents without known chronic illness were drawn from freshman volunteers who were attending a suburban high school.

More detailed descriptions of the samples and the procedures used for their assessment can be found elsewhere (8–10).

The Interviews

Adolescents were interviewed yearly by trained mental health professionals (psychiatrists, psychologists, or psychiatric social workers). The interview style was exploratory, using open-ended questions. Several topics were covered, including school and home life, peer relationships, illness experiences, and hopes for the future. One related topic cut across all others: the ways in which conflicts, affects, and external crises were perceived and handled by the subject. This interview, therefore, covered a broad range of concerns relevant to the adolescent subject in a manner similar to an initial, open-ended, clinical interview. While the interviewers sought to explore various aspects of the adolescent's life experience, individual interviews differed in the extent to which certain topics were covered. The coverage variations stemmed from the adolescent's own areas of special interest or concern, which were explored in more depth as determined by the capacity of the subject. For example, the presence of parental conflicts and divorce often led to prolonged discussions of the family and the subject's own concerns and coping patterns in response to this problem area.

The interviews were audiotaped and transcribed. The transcripts served as the material from which ego defenses were rated.

The Defense Codes

In order to generate an inclusive set of ego defenses with usable definitions, we reviewed relevant literature, most especially the work of A. Freud (1), Valenstein and colleagues (15), Prelinger and Zimet (14), and Vaillant (6). Valenstein's work, in particular, provided us with conceptually oriented definitions of defense mechanisms. From these sources, we selected defenses that were widely recognized and pertinent for a population of adolescents. Currently, we assess subjects by means of ratings of 12 defenses. In addition, we have established a separate code for overall defensive success. (See Table 1.) Some other defenses included in earlier versions of our coding manual were excluded subsequently for various reasons. As an example, identification with the aggressor and identification with the lost object were initially included. The definitions of these defenses required the coder to determine the object with whom the subject was identifying, which proved extremely difficult from a single interview. We also excluded defenses such as those used by patients with borderline character disorders. This decision stemmed more from our focus on adolescent development rather than from any particular view of the overall merits of these particular defenses. We believe that our approach could be used to develop other defense codes—for example, for rating defenses used by patients with severe character disorders.

While definitions used by the Valenstein group (15) and others provided a major starting point for our codes, we have refined them in three ways. 1) Where definitions were confusing, changes were made in the definitions themselves. 2) Based on Prelinger's and Zimet's approach, we developed a five-point scale of intensity from minimally present to strongly and intensively present. Brief descriptions were provided for each major point on the scale. 3) From a subset of our interviews we then generated case examples for each scale point. Part V of the Appendix, which presents a glossary of the conceptual definitions for each of the defenses taken from our unpublished manual also gives examples of the approach, using the defense of ascetisim.

Table 1. Reliabilities for Defense Codes

	Intraclass Correlations
Acting out	.69
Altruism	.54
Asceticism	.76
Avoidance	.67
Denial	.37
Displacement	.74
Intellectualization	.56
Projection	.32
Rationalization	.38
Repression	.46
Suppression	.62
Turning against self	.67
Overall	.60

Using the combination of a definition, specified scale points, and examples, raters judge each subject on all defenses. They can withhold ratings on the presence of specific defenses if sufficient information is lacking, but in practice this has occurred very infrequently (16). Raters are instructed to use the entire interview to make each rating. Thus, the rater uses both the frequency of episodes found in the entire interview and the strength of a particular vignette to judge the subject. For example, in the illustrations given in part V of the Appendix, the subject who was rated as using a moderate level of asceticism presented different instances of relatively subtle ascetic responses. If she had shown only one, stronger instance of ascetic attitudes, such as strong disgust over sexual activity, this could also be rated as a moderate level of asceticism. The subject examples rated as showing higher levels of asceticism demonstrated more frequent strong instances of ascetic attitudes.

In each rating, information derives from both interview behavior and self-reports of the subject. For example, altruism may be shown both through charitable actions to friends and by specific attempts to be helpful in providing information to the interviewer. Acting out may be identified through reports by the subject as well as by impulsivity motivated by anxiety during the interview.

Reliability of the Defenses Codes

On a subset of 18 transcripts, interrater reliability was assessed (three raters were compared) for all codes using the intraclass correlation statistic (18). The sample size for the three-way reliability study was selected with statistical consultation (Bartko J., personal communication, 1982). Table 1 shows the defenses and the intraclass correlation reliabilities. Based on previously developed guidelines for evaluating intraclass correlations (19), three of the 13 codes showed fair levels of agreement (.004–0.59); five showed good levels of agreement (0.60–0.74); and one showed an excellent level of agreement (0.75–1.00). These findings suggest that on the whole these codes can be reliably used by trained coders.

We have now also trained two additional sets of raters to use these codes. Although these raters ranged widely in clinical experience and training, their levels of reliability were quite similar to those presented here. This suggests that these defense codes can be taught and used by other groups interested in evaluating defense profiles from clinical interviews.

However, our own experience with these codes indicates that certain problems interfere with their reliable use. These stem in part from the theory of defenses and its application to clinical material. A major problem is that raters have widely different expectations about the level of speculation that should be invoked. The trained clinician often looks for subtle cues on which to hypothesize the presence of certain conflicts and defensive processes. This serves the clinician well in actual practice but can create problems in coding reliably, where a turn of phrase can be interpreted in many distinct ways. The case examples are particularly useful in moderating the amount of inference used in evaluating defenses. By providing brief descriptions of how subjects have been rated, we think the degree of speculation is decreased. Thus, after reading a transcript, the coder reviews each code definition and rates the subject on that scale. Then, using the examples, the rater reviews the decision. This approach parallels the method of scoring used by Loevinger and colleagues in developing the Washington University Sentence Completion Test of ego development, and has led to acceptable levels of interrater reliability for the use of their instrument by many different groups of investigators (20, 21).

COMMENT

In this chapter we have suggested that many of our scales for measuring defenses show acceptable levels of reliability. If reliable, is there evidence that these ratings capture meaningful psychological processes? In more scientific terms, is there evidence for their validity? In an unpublished companion manuscript, we have presented findings that do support the validity of these ratings. In that paper we report that there were substantial differences in defense usage in the psychiatric adolescents we have studied in comparison to the diabetic and healthy adolescents. For example, the psychiatric adolescents were higher in use of such defenses as acting out, avoidance, displacement, projection, and turning against self, and lower in use of altruism, asceticism, suppression, and intellectualization.

We also compared defense usage to ego development level as assessed by Loevinger's sentence completion test (21, 22). The patterns of defense-ego development correlations follow expectations, in that defenses such as projection, acting out, denial, and avoidance show negative correlations with high ego development levels, and defenses such as altruism, intellectualization, and suppression show positive correlations with high ego development level. These findings suggest that our scales are sufficiently sensitive to detect adolescents at different levels of development and psychopathology. Currently, we are exploring the role of defense usage in maintenance of self-esteem. While preliminary, this work also suggests that defenses that are positively associated with ego development level are also linked to higher self-esteem.

In conclusion, we have presented an approach to the systematic assessment of ego defenses from in-depth exploratory interviews. This approach to the coding of development and the use of defense mechanisms may be useful in several areas of psychiatry, including studies of adolescent development and evaluation of change during psychotherapy. Systematizing measurements of defenses and other concepts derived from psychoanalysis may also be useful in training therapists.

References

1. Melville H: Moby Dick. New York, Random House, 1950

2. Freud A: The Ego and the Mechanisms of Defense (1937). New York, International Universities Press, 1966

3. Freud S: Inhibitions, symptoms and anxiety (1926), in The Complete Psychological Works, vol. 20. Translated by Strachey J. London, Hogarth Press, 1953

4. Bond M, Gardner ST, Christian J, et al: Empirical study of self-rated defense styles. Arch Gen Psychiatry 40:333-338, 1983

5. Haan N: Coping and Defending. San Francisco, Jossey-Bass, 1977

6. Vaillant GE: Adaptation to Life. Boston, Little, Brown, 1977

7. Klerman GL, Vaillant GE, Spitzer RL, et al: A debate on *DSM-III*. Am J Psychiatry 141:539-553, 1984

8. Hauser ST, Jacobson AM, Noam G, et al: Ego development and self-image complexity in early adolescence: longitudinal studies of psychiatric and diabetic patients. Arch Gen Psychiatry 40:32-33, 1983

9. Jacobson AM, Hauser ST, Powers S, et al: The influences of chronic illness and ego development level on self-esteem in diabetic and psychiatric patients. J Youth Adolescence 13:489-507, 1984

10. Jacobson AM, Hauser ST, Powers S, et al: Ego development in diabetics: a longitudinal study, in Psychological Aspects of Diabetes in Children and Adolescents. Edited by Laron A, Galatzer A. Basel, Karger, 1983

11. Gleser GD, Ihilevich D: An objective instrument for measuring defense mechanisms. J Consult Clin Psychol 33:51-60, 1969

12. Grinker RR, Weble B, Drye R: The Borderline Syndrome. New York, Basic Books, 1968

13. Semrad EV, Grinspoon L, Feinberg SE: Development of an ego profile scale. Arch Gen Psychiatry 28:70-77, 1973

14. Prelinger E, Zimet C: An Ego Psychological Approach to Character Assessment. Glenco, IL, Free Press, 1964

15. Bibring G, Dwyer T, Huntington D, et al: A study of the psychological processes in pregnancy and of the earliest mother-child relationship, II. Psychoanal Study Child 16:25-72, 1961

16. Jacobson A, Beardslee W, Hauser ST, et al: Assessing adolescent ego processes. Scientific Proceedings, American Psychiatric Association 135:51, 1982

17. Beardslee W, Jacobson AM, Hauser ST, et al: An approach to evaluating adolescent adaptive processes: scale development and reliability. J Am Acad Child Psychol 24:637-642, 1985

18. Bartko J, Carpenter W: On the methods and theory of reliability. J Nerv Ment Dis 16:307-317, 1976

19. Cichetti D, Sparrow S: The Behavioral Inventory for Rating Development (BIRD). Proceedings of the Social Statistics Section, American Statistical Association, 218-223, 1982

20. Loevinger J, Wessler R: Measuring Ego Development. Vol. 1. San Francisco, Jossey-Bass, 1970

21. Loevinger J, Wessler R, Redmore D: Measuring Ego Development. Vol. 2, Scoring Manual for Women and Girls. San Francisco, Jossey-Bass, 1970

4

Toward Reliability in Identifying Ego Defenses Through Verbal Behavior

Leigh McCullough, Ph.D.
Caroline O. Vaillant, M.S.S.W.
George E. Vaillant, M.D.

4

Toward Reliability in Identifying Ego Defenses Through Verbal Behavior

Like the authors of the other chapters, we are concerned by the lack of methods for objective measurement of ego defenses, which has impeded their empirical verification. As indicated, taxonomies of ego defenses have been developed (1–3), but a reliable methodology for labelling and distinguishing defensive behaviors has been difficult to achieve. The problem with achieving the goals of reliable identification of defenses is threefold: 1) ego defenses are intrapsychic constructs; 2) the specific behaviors that identify these mental dispositions are widely heterogeneous, and no single behavior is either necessary or sufficient to identify a defense; 3) different raters view and code defenses from different perspectives, so that what may appear to be defensive behavior to one rater may not appear so to another. Thus, traditional methods of item-by-item identification are not applicable here.

To the untrained observer all deciduous trees look alike. To distinguish the maple from the oak, one must learn the differences in, for example, type of leaf or type of bark. Likewise, to the untrained eye, the behavior manifestations known as ego defenses might appear as quirks, eccentricities, or just plain personality traits. A reliable classification system would allow the differential distinction of the constructs that are inferred from such behavioral manifestations into discrete defenses. But, alas, leaves and trees can be seen, touched, and examined, while ego defenses will ever remain hypothetical constructs.

In an impressive discussion of how to make intrapsychic constructs admissible to scientific study, Zuriff (4) has suggested a possible solution. He reminds us that the Wittgensteinian concept for family resemblance might be a fruitful approach here. Looking at a photograph of a large family, one may note that although not every family member has the same eyes, nose or mouth, there is a similarity of features. Most family members share the same resemblance, even though there is no one feature that characterizes each and every member. Thus, reliability can be achieved in heterogeneous samples by a consensus of agreement regarding their resemblance to an inferred construct.

The goal of this chapter is to work toward shortening the empirical distance between manifest behavior and hypothesized underlying mechanisms by consensus of agreement across raters. First, we will define the concept of ego defenses that we are using. Then the results of a reliability study will be presented with specific examples of defensive behavior found in the case histories of the Grant Study of Adult Development (5).

DEFINITION

Defenses may be defined as intrapsychic coping mechanisms that have the function of keeping anxiety within manageable limits. In contrast to "coping skills," a term used by behaviorists for techniques that are taught to help a patient voluntarily manage anxiety, deployment of defenses is not voluntary. We hypothesize that ego defenses represent certain unconscious cognitive "distortions" of internal and external reality, varying from person to person, that are reinforced when they serve to diminish cognitive dissonance and dysphoria resulting from sudden changes in the internal and external milieu.

An inherent difficulty in reliably identifying defenses is that what may be a defense in one context may not be defensive in another. For example, the act of forgetting can be a manifestation of active repression of a painful stimulus, or it may indicate the normal decay of a memory trace. Thus, in order to decide that a defense is present, one must make assumptions about the internal state or motivation of the subject. Furthermore, the identification of defenses is often influenced by the personality (or defenses) of the viewer. These obstacles to reliability will be discussed in regard to the examples found in the case histories.

METHODS

Vaillant's hierarchy of defenses (see part III of the Appendix) was used as the guiding conceptual model to identify ego defenses in case histories from a longitudinal study of college men. Two independent raters were trained to over .80 reliability criterion (r = .82 for specific defenses; r = .95 for overall defensive style) on approximately 150 examples of defenses embedded in 10 interview reports. Then, each rater read and coded seven extensive case histories spanning the past 40 years, which included not only research interviews but also biannual self-report questionnaires. There were roughly 300 pages of data in each case dossier.

Each rater's objective was to find examples of defensive behavior in the verbal statements, quotes, excerpts, or descriptions of behavior in the subject's record. The problem that faced these raters was that vignettes were not preselected. Hundreds of pages of unstructured descriptive information in several forms (self-report, significant-other report, research interviews, etc.) were contained in bulky, aging file folders. The raters had the challenge of reviewing this varied material, trying to select the most salient examples, and then deciding which of 18 defense labels best fit each example. To achieve reliability, the independent raters would have to not only assign the same labels to a given example but also select the same example. This is a far more stringent test of rater reliability than exists in most clinical studies.

RESULTS

A total of 517 examples were gleaned by the two raters from the seven cases for an average of 73.8 examples per case (range = 32 to

87). In 324 instances the two raters both identified the same example. An additional 193 examples were identified by either one or the other of the two raters but not by both. Rater A identified 68, and Rater B identified 125 such examples. Thus, the raters agreed in item selection for 63 percent of the examples selected (Table 1).

Of the 324 examples listed by both raters, there was agreement about specific defenses (that is, repression, suppression, and the like) on 214 or 66 percent. When the specific defenses were clustered into their hierarchical categories (the immature, intermediate, and mature categories in part III, Appendix), the agreement between raters increased to 254 cases or 78 percent.

Table 2 presents the level of agreement of the two raters on specific defense mechanisms. The raters showed greater reliability on mature defenses (only 13 percent disagreements) than on intermediate or immature defenses (44 percent and 43 percent respectively). In assessing the rate of disagreements, it must be realized that by chance raters would agree in only seven percent of cases.

Disagreements on defenses provide an opportunity to isolate problems in coding. Taking into consideration only the examples identified by both raters, the four defenses in Table 2 that were most agreed upon (percent agreement of total items coded) were suppression, altruism, acting out, and repression. The five defenses

Table 1. Breakdown of Defenses Coded by Two Raters, According to Identification of Items and to Agreement on Examples

A. Agreement on Identification of Items		
Examples identified by both raters:	324	(63%)
Examples identified only by rater A:	68	(13%)
Examples identified only by rater B:	125	(24%)
Total different examples identified in seven charts:	517	(100%)
B. Agreement on Categories of Defense Among the 324 Examples		
Agreement: 254 examples (78%)		
Disagreement: 70 examples (22%)		
C. Agreement on Specific Defenses Among the 324 Examples		
Agreement: 214 examples (66%)		
Disagreement: 110 examples (34%)		

that were least agreed upon were sublimation, dissociation, reaction formation, displacement, and hypochondriasis.

There seemed to be three major reasons for high disagreement: lack of clinical salience, "close relatives" among the defenses, and rater idiosyncrasy. First, counting the ratings made by each rater separately, in the seven cases only nine examples of reaction formation and six of hypochondriasis were noted. Thus, lack of agreement here may have simply meant that these mechanisms were not dominant styles used by the seven individuals whose cases were analyzed.

Table 2. Agreement Between the Two Raters in Labelling Those Examples That Both Identified as Reflecting Defensive Behaviors

	Agreements (N = 214 examples)	Disagreements (N = 110 examples)
Suppression	22	4
Altruism	11	2
Anticipation	2	1
Sublimation	3	6 (!)
Humor	5	0
Total mature defenses	43 pairs (87%)	13 examples (13%)
Repression	15	7
Reaction formation	1	7 (!)
Intellectualization	17	12
Displacement	4	30 (!)
Total intermediate defenses	37 pairs (57%)	56 examples (44%)
Dissociation	4	16 (!)
Hypochondriasis	0	6 (!)
Schizoid fantasy	6	4
Acting out	3	1
Passive aggressive	12	11
Projection	2	2
Mild Denial	0	1
Total immature defenses	27 pairs (57%)	41 examples (43%)
Totals	214 examples (107 agreement pairs)	110 examples

(!) = one of five least agreed-upon defenses.

Second, displacement provided an example of a defense with several "close relatives." Of 30 instances where one rater coded an item displacement, the other rater coded it as sublimation (six times), intellectualization (five times), dissociation (five times), hypochondriasis (four times), and some other defense (10 times). Three of the four alternative defenses are conceptually closely related to displacement. Sublimation is the "mature" defense most closely related to displacement, and hypochondriasis is the closest "immature" defense. In obsessional patients intellectualization (isolation of affect) and displacement are commonly paired. The explanation for disagreement about the defense was not that one rater idiosyncratically favored displacement. Rather, the rater apparently disagreed more because of the problem of definition and because displacement can take so many forms. Thus, the importance of sharpening criteria to achieve mutually exclusive definitions is underscored. This point is emphasized by other chapters in this monograph.

The third cause of rater unreliability, rater idiosyncracy, was apparent with regard to dissociation. Of the 16 disagreements, 13 were coded as dissociation by Rater A and only three were coded as dissociation by Rater B. Additional clarification of definition and better training are required here.

To illustrate some of the specific issues addressed above, two defenses will be presented with brief definitions and examples of agreements and disagreements from the case records. One example will be drawn from one of the most agreed-upon defenses, repression, and the other from one of the most disagreed-upon defenses, displacement.

CASE EXAMPLES

Repression

Definition: Seemingly inexplicable naiveté, memory lapse, or failure to acknowledge input from a selected sense organ. Repression is a defense that protects the subject from being aware of what he or she is feeling. The emotional elements are clearly experi-

enced, but the cognitive elements remain outside of consciousness. Repeated responses to questions such as, "I don't know," "I
can't remember," "My mind goes blank," or not acknowledging
the obvious.

Case Examples from a Single Person:

1. Said "I don't know" to everything. When asked "Was your
   career a poor choice?" he replied, "Yes—but I'm not sure why I
   said yes."

2. (Later) "I don't know why I drifted into engineering. I might
   be happy with it—but I'm not at all sure."

3. (Question) "What are your beliefs over rough spots?" (Answer) "How does anyone answer that question? I'm afraid I
   don't know."

4. (Question) "Have you met your expectations 20 years after
   college?" (Answer) "I haven't the slightest idea what I expected 20 years ago."

5. (Question) "Is sexual tension a problem?" (Answer) "Damned
   if I know—unless it is subconscious."

6. He reported that he loses his temper frequently, but can't
   remember even one incident.

7. (Question) "What do you do in your spare time?" (Answer)
   "Questions like this make me wonder what I do—I don't
   have any idea—I seem to keep busy."

8. (Question) "What do you do over rough spots?" (Answer) "I
   don't know what you mean. I haven't had any." (But he had!)

9. (Shortly after World War II) "I can't say how the danger
   affected me. I guess I'm still reacting."

10. "I can't remember whether I had sexual thoughts as a boy."

11. "The way I handle problems is to forget them."

Repression, more broadly defined, plays a part in many other
defenses. We tried to code repression only when it stood alone.

Furthermore, in self-report data, it is often unclear whether the subject was consciously withholding information from us when an "I don't know" or "I'm not sure" answer was given, or whether the information reflects genuine repression. Clearly, redundancy, as in the example above, provided the only assurance. Clinical salience is as important to raters of defenses as it is in biography.

Displacement

Definition: The redirection of feelings toward a relatively less cared-for object. Displacement refers to the expression of an affect, impulse or action toward a person, object or bodily part other than the one that initially aroused the affect or feeling. The affect is fully acknowledged but is redirected to a less conflictual target.

Two sets of behavioral examples associated with displacement will be presented below, categorized by the targets to which they are directed and the valence they carry. On the first set of examples, the raters agreed.

Displacement Toward Objects:

1. "I was so mad that I went out and slammed a tennis ball." (But if the subject reported winning tennis tournaments or feeling the thrill of competition, this would be coded sublimation.)
2. "When work goes bad I blow off steam in my garden." (If working in the garden were a mindless way of escaping work problems *without acknowledging the anger*, this would be coded dissociation. And, as in the tennis example above, if while gardening the subject created something of beauty rather than merely hacking at the ground, this could be coded sublimation.)

Bodily Ailments Under Stress:

1. "I got a terrific headache after the boss yelled at me."
2. "During that bad year at work, I ended up with chronic indigestion."

Displacement Through Wit or Sarcasm:

1. "At one time I was drinking so much I could have put the National Distillers on a second shift!" (The subject is his own target in this example.)
2. "When the subject was asked if he ever had psychiatric treatment, he wrote (to the Grant Study psychiatrist), "Anyone who goes to a psychiatrist should have his head examined." (These examples are distinguished from humor, in which no one is attacked.)

Displacement of Positive Feelings:

1. "We treat our dog like the child we don't have. . . . We are even taking Rover to Europe this summer!"

Displacement was one of the defenses for which we initially had difficulty in obtaining reliability, and was one of the most disagreed-upon defenses in this study. As evident in the varied list of behaviors above, the human mind is capable of great diversity in directing emotion toward multiple targets. First, there are multiple objects: people, places, body parts, and things. Second, there are also multiple ways to displace, running the gamut of emotion: anger (criticism), apparent "humor" (wit or sarcasm), fears or phobias (anxiety). When is prejudice projection and when is it displacement? When is play displacement and when is it sublimation? These can be fine distinctions. Below are some examples on which the raters disagreed.

1. "I am extremely happy doing surgery." (Is this creative fulfillment or displaced aggression?)

2. As a boy, the subject always mercilessly teased his sister. (This was coded passive–aggressive by one rater and as displacement by the other. Could it not be both?)

3. "I am not excited by my life's work, but this doesn't bother me a bit." (One rater coded this dissociation and the other coded it reaction formation. Like #2, it has components of both.)

The above examples do not really provide sufficient data to make the necessary distinctions. More data are required so that patterns in defensive style can be determined by consensus rather than by item agreement, and this brings us to a second important point.

In coding these case histories, what we were seeking was agreement on the overall pattern of behavior. Reliability is usually established on a predetermined set of items, but data in this report were generated from unstructured cases. As with facial recognition or hidden figures, individual raters may not base judgments on identical groups of stimuli, but they may agree on the family nonetheless. Defensive behaviors reflect fragments of personality just as nose and eyes reflect parts of the face. Thus, in Table 1, 193 examples of defenses were coded by either Rater A or Rater B but not by both. However, 56 percent of the individually identified examples by Rater B illustrated defensive styles already identified as a predominant style for a given individual by Rater A. Thus, in coding defenses one objective may be to arrive at consensus by redundancy, not certainty, for each single item. Reliability on every item can only be achieved by standardized stimuli, and the study of defenses occurs in the wilds, not the laboratory.

CONCLUSION

The surface event (recorded verbal behavior) will never totally represent a complex, multifaceted intrapsychic state of mind. When we try to squeeze science out of art, some of the beauty and mystery is lost. On the other hand, what is gained is evidence that we can get our hands on and test by consensual validation. Popper has said that the best we can ever achieve is a "woven web of conjectures." This chapter has attempted to weave the conjectural web for ego defenses somewhat tighter.

In our efforts to rate relative maturity of defensive behavior, we intentionally cast a wide net. The trade-off was the increased likelihood of false positives. For example, we knew that all cases of "I don't know" in response to personal questions did not represent repression. But clinical experience suggests that high frequency of

"I don't knows" does correlate with repression. The check on our inclusive style of rating was redundancy. Consensus was necessary before a choice was considered significant.

References

1. Freud A: The Ego and the Mechanisms of Defense (1937). New York, International Universities Press, 1966

2. Vaillant GE: Theoretical hierarchy of adaptive ego mechanisms. Arch Gen Psychiatry 24:107-118, 1971

3. Meissner WW, Mack JE: Theories of personality and psychopathology: classical psychoanalysis, in Comprehensive Textbook of Psychiatry, II. Edited by Freedman AM, Kaplan HI. Baltimore, Williams and Wilkins, 1975

4. Zuriff G: Behaviorism: A Conceptual Reconstruction. New York, Columbia University Press, 1985

5. Vaillant G: Adaptation to Life. Boston, Little, Brown, 1977

5

A Cross-Validation Of Two Empirical Studies of Defenses

George E. Vaillant, M.D.
Caroline O. Vaillant, M.S.S.W.

5

A Cross-Validation Of
Two Empirical Studies
of Defenses

In Chapter 1, Bond reports on the value of his self-administered questionnaire, which taps possible conscious derivatives of defenses. By using factor analysis, Bond demonstrated that statements selected to reflect relatively mature and immature defenses were significantly correlated with mental health and maturity of ego development (as measured by Loevinger's (1) sentence completion test). His instrument has the obvious advantages of being free from subjective clinical judgment and free from halo and context effects. However, Bond did not demonstrate the capacity of his questionnaire to identify individual defenses. Nor did he provide clinical corroboration of his subjects' judgments about their defenses.

In the Introduction, I referred to my own efforts to validate a hierarchy of defenses on college men and to a replication study based on a sample of socially disadvantaged men (2). In the latter study maturity of individual defensive styles correlated highly with independent and objective measures of mental health, and rater-reliability for overall maturity of defensive style was .84. However, if the difficulty with pencil and paper instruments is that their validity is less easy to prove than their reliability, the difficulty with clinical methods is that reliability is often suspect because of observer bias. In my work, reliable clinical identification of defenses could only be achieved when the rater knew as much as possible about the subject's inner and outer reality. The problem, then, becomes how to prove that the observed correlation of defensive style with outcome was not the result of the nonblind rating condition.

Because I thought that a possible solution to the complementary limitations of these two methods was to combine them, I administered Bond's context-free questionnaire to my subjects, whose functioning in the real world had been assessed for four decades. First, if Bond's theoretically derived statements correlated with clinical identification of the same defenses, his use of self-report would be validated. Second, if Bond's statements, created to identify specific defensive styles, in fact correlated with independent clinical assessments of those defensive styles, that would provide evidence that Vaillant's raters were not making their judgments on the basis of halo effects. Third, since Bond's questionnaire was administered in 1983, six to eight years after the interviews on which the clinical assessments of defenses were based, significant correlations would also provide empirical support for the long-standing belief that defenses represent trait-like facets of personality. Recently this belief has been called into question by Brenner, who asserts, "No one's repertory of defense is limited or repetitive" (3, p. 569).

SUBJECTS AND METHODS

Subjects were drawn from the 456 school boys who had been chosen as controls for the Gluecks' (4) study of delinquency. These men have been followed prospectively for 40 years (5). The sub-sample in this chapter included 131 subjects who at an average age of 54 ± 2 completed Bond's self-report questionnaire. All subjects were white males. Fifty percent had not graduated from high school, and their mean IQ was 97 ± 12.

MEASURES

Health-Sickness Rating Scale (HSRS)

The HSRS (6) assesses global mental health by placing individuals on a continuum from 1 to 100 in which institutional dependency receives a rating of 0–25 and multiple manifestations of positive mental health receive a rating of 90–100. Rater reliability was .89. The subjects had been assessed when the men had been interviewed at age 47 ± 2.

Maturity (Health) of Defenses (Adaptive Style)

The definitions of the individual defenses are provided in Appendix, part III. The empirical rationale for equating "maturity" of defensive style with both developmental maturity and freedom from psychopathology is provided elsewhere (8). "Healthy" may be a more accurate term than "mature," but "mature" captures the fact that as young adults grow older or recover from mental illness, their choice of defenses evolves along the hierarchy outlined in the following paragraph.

Raters of defenses were blinded both to childhood records and to independent adult ratings. They were given uniform definitions of 15 defenses and trained on interview protocols that had been rated by many others. The 15 defenses were divided into three clusters determined on the basis of prior empirical study: 1) Mature (sublimation, suppression, anticipation, altruism, and humor); 2) Intermediate/neurotic (displacement, repression, isolation [intellectualization], and reaction formation); and 3) Immature (projection, schizoid fantasy, passive aggression [turning against the self], acting out, hypochondriasis, and dissociation [neurotic denial]). Raters were given a 20- to 30-page summary of the men's two-hour semi-structured interview at age 47. These interviews had been designed to focus on difficulties in the individual's relationships, physical health, and work. In writing the interview summary, the interviewer was instructed to elucidate but not to label the behaviors by which the individuals had coped with these difficulties. Interview protocols were prepared by the interviewer from verbatim notes taken during the interview. Numerous direct quotes were included in the interview protocols, but the methodology embodied both the scientific limitations and advantages of journalism. The purpose was to use the interviewer's summary as the first step in data reduction and to retain interview emphasis often lost in transcripts of tape recordings.

For each of the interview protocols, raters were asked to note *all possible* instances of each of the 15 defensive styles. Attention was paid to concrete past behaviors, to style of adaptation to past difficulties, and to specific vicissitudes of the interview interaction.

In order to control for variation across subjects in the frequency of identified defensive vignettes, the following quantitative strategy was adopted, forcing clinical judgment of the global maturity (health) of defenses into a nine-point scale. The relative proportion of defense vignettes in each of the three general categories— mature, intermediate, immature—was determined. This ratio was used to distribute a total of eight points. Of the eight points, one to five points were assigned to each of the three general categories, but the total had to be eight. The score for overall defensive style for each man was then estimated by subtracting the rating (1–5) for immature defenses from the rating (1–5) for mature defenses. This procedure provided a nine-point range, a normal distribution of scores by both raters, and a rater reliability of .84. Global ratings by the two raters differed by more than two points for only 23 subjects (seven percent). (In calculating global maturity of defenses, the intermediate category was ignored; the rationale for ignoring this category is its insignificant correlation with outcome variables. See Table 1, Introduction.)

Individual Defenses

For each interview, 10 to 30 instances of defensive behavior were noted, reflecting three to seven different defenses. Weighting of the salience of each individual defense was achieved through *redundancy*—that is, through frequency rather than certainty of identification. Each rater scored each defense: zero if absent, 1 if noted once or twice, 2 if it was the most frequently used defense or noted three times or more. Reliability was only modest. The raters had more difficulty agreeing on individual defense ratings, and depending on the defense, one rater could score a given defense 2 (major) and the other could score it zero (absent) in four to 20 percent of cases. The two raters' ratings were summed, providing an individual rating for each defense that ranged from zero (both agreed it was absent) to 4 (both agreed it was major).

Clinical Illustration. Evidence by which two men each received a 4 on suppression (a mature defense) is contrasted with the evidence by which two men received a 4 on schizoid fantasy (an immature defense). These particular defenses were chosen both because they were the most highly correlated, positively and negatively, with objective evidence of mental health and because they were among the most conceptually difficult of the defenses. The examples illustrate the inferred intrapsychic mechanisms, the objective criteria that the blind raters excerpted from the interview protocols in order to rate the subjects, and the use of repetition to make clinical judgments. The subjects' social class of origin, their education, and their assessed childhood environment were not significantly associated with maturity of defenses.

In brief, schizoid fantasy was defined as creating gratifying interpersonal relationships inside one's head that had little counterpart in reality; suppression was defined as stoicism, minimizing but not denying distress, and postponing gratification without denying or repressing the experienced affect.

Case A. Schizoid Fantasy (11 grades of school, good childhood environment, parents in social class V)

This man works as a library clerk. He enjoys a vicarious sense of prestigiousness from the slight association that he has with professors and doctors. "I just like the academic atmosphere . . . ," he said. "I just sort of feel a part of it." When asked about his future, "I will still be at the library, maybe something on the academic level. I'm still interested in photography. . . . I've had so many cameras." He talked with a tinge of grandiosity as he began to talk about certain cousins in the "old country" who were all "eight feet tall." At age 47 and unmarried, he blamed religious prejudice. He said he had had little to do with non-Jewish girls. When asked about relationships with women, he recalled a girl at school 35 years ago, in 1942, on whom he had had a crush and of whom he had thoughts of marrying. He thought that she had married someone else. There had been no one since. He does not drive or have a driver's license, but he said he might be interested in getting a license in the future. He said he knew "intuitively" how to drive a car and did not require driving lessons. He does not entertain much but relaxes in his spare time, listening to the radio or records by himself.

Case B. Schizoid Fantasy (9 grades of school, childhood environment only fair, parents in social class IV)

This man works as a night security guard. He entered into it for "no special reason" but because he was "fascinated by it." When asked of any difficulty in the job he remarked that alertness is the top priority. He said he gets along with people and illustrated this by a story of striking up a conversation with people on a park bench during a vacation in California. Mostly he works alone. If living his life over, he thought he might be a physical therapist or a lawyer because he wanted to help people. He was interested in journalism, and he occasionally thought of writing a book. He took an electronics course, but nothing came of it. He said that his family is very close-knit. Actually, his parents were divorced 25 years ago; recently they had remarried each other but lived 2000 miles away. He said he was not particularly close to any one relative. "They are all the same—cousins, aunts, and everybody." He had had no children. Then he said if he had had children, he imagines that he might have had a son killed in Viet Nam or a "daughter to worry me sick." Instead, he and his wife have a dog and a cat. He said of his dog, "You could swear that he was human." He said of his cat, "He has a mind of his own." He and his wife get along although he said they should not because he is a Scorpio and she is a Leo. When troubled or angry, he runs up to the attic to listen to his citizen's band radio, which has a police scanner. After five or ten minutes, his anger passes. He never did have a special friend. He said that he is not a loner but that he just doesn't happen to see anyone. There is no one outside his family to whom he would go for help because he "never needs people." He and his wife mostly "keep to ourselves" and "don't need anyone." His hobbies include CB radio, photography, shooting targets (not animals), and fishing. He also likes war movies.

Case C. Suppression (11 grades of school, childhood environment only fair, parents in social class IV)

His main job is "keeping the peace between customers and the boss,"
and he finds he often has to "bite his tongue" in his role as diplomat.
  He has been married for 26 years and said "nothing really bothers
him" about his wife. "She's my whole life. I get to love her more
every day. . . . The family just doesn't disagree about much . . . nothing major." He and his wife both agree that they have worked hard on
their marriage but "after 26 years it's beautiful." He and his wife
remember that they had thought of separating in the first year of their
marriage.
  When he feels bad, he tries to "think positive," and then he tries to
"take care of whatever the problem is." For instance, when he is
overwhelmed with bills, he just starts to pay them one at a time.
Fearing alcoholism, he stopped drinking 19 years ago and has been
abstinent since.
  He said he hasn't been sick a day in his life. Hearing this, his wife
groaned and said, "He would go to work even if he was bleeding."
When he gets a cold, he doesn't believe in staying home as he always
says "I have to work."

Case D. Suppression (9 grades of school, childhood environment
only fair, parents in social class V)

This man was not able to report having had any serious problems with
other men in his shop. When he gets troubled, he tries not to show it
and "to take things in stride." In this way, he maintains an even
temperament, "at least on the outside." At work he is known as the
man with "no emotions" because he never looks rattled. "I want to
make sure I know what I am hollering about before I start hollering."
"I guess I just don't want to make a fool of myself—if you get mad first
and then find out you're wrong, well, then it's too late." He did
speculate first that his style might have been the reason for his ulcer
problem. When he is especially troubled, he talks things over with his
wife and they try to settle it together. When he gets very angry, he
becomes quiet. He never raises his voice and tries to avoid blowing his
top. Sometimes he will sit and play music on his record player until he
cools off. He generally tries to avoid fights. On the other hand, he says
that he never backed down from a fight if it got to a point where it
could not be avoided without losing face.

I want to emphasize three points by means of these vignettes. First, suppression looks so reasonable that it is hard to imagine that it is not voluntary until one reflects that if conscious coping with stress were that easy, more people would use suppression. Second, the inferred intrapsychic mechanisms are based on behaviors that do not just reflect success or failure at working and loving. They have more to do with cognitive and affective styles than with the instrumental behaviors on which outcome ratings were based. Third, when asked to explain their defensive behavior, all subjects could be said to use rationalization. What determines defense identification is the actual behavior, not the subject's explanation of that behavior.

Bond Defense Style Questionnaire

As indicated, the questionnaire (9) was administered when the men were 54 ± 2 years and was designed to elicit manifestations of a subject's characteristic style of dealing with conflict, whether conscious or unconscious. It is based on the assumption that persons can accurately comment on their behavior from a distance. Subjects were asked to indicate their degree of agreement or disagreement with 67 statements (those marked with an asterisk in part VI of the Appendix) on a five-point scale (1 = strongly disagree; 5 = strongly agree). Some of the 15 defenses I cited were not listed by Bond, and in addition to the defenses in my study, Bond designed his statements to reflect behavior suggestive of pseudoaltruism, as-if behavior, clinging, regression, somatization, withdrawal, omnipotence–devaluation, inhibition, identification, primitive idealization, and splitting.

Because the current project was designed to correlate Vaillant's hierarchy of defenses with Bond's questionnaire, each of 67 Bond statements was relabeled to reflect one of Vaillant's 15 defense mechanisms. Labels reflected the consensus of three raters. In 44 items the labels were the same as Bond's. In 23, statements originally selected to reflect defense terms favored by Otto Kernberg and Melanie Klein were translated into those used by Vaillant (usually passive aggression, fantasy, or projection). Both groups of investigators agreed that the remaining 10 statements constituted a lie scale. The final theoretical labels for statements included 42 statements reflecting immature defenses (11 = projection, 10 = passive aggression, 7 = fantasy, 5 = dissociation, 4 = acting out, 2 = hypochondriasis, and 3 = unclassified). Nine statements reflected neurotic or intermediate defenses (7 = reaction formation, 1 = displacement, and 1 = isolation), and six reflected mature mechanisms (2 = suppression, 2 = humor, 1 = sublimation, 1 = altruism). (Bond's Factor I had been made up exclusively of statements associated with immature defenses, and Bond's Factor IV was made up exclusively of statements reflecting mature defenses.)

RESULTS

Judgment of defensive style required extensive information regarding the men's lives, including their capacity to work and to love. There was no way of completely blinding the raters of defensive behavior from the behaviors underlying the ratings of the outcome variables. Thus, halo effects could be controlled only by finding an independent means of assessing defenses, in this case the Bond questionnaire.

Only 307 of the 456 subjects could be reliably rated for defenses at age 47. Of these 307, about seven years later, 131 returned the Bond questionnaire. The 131 who returned the Bond questionnaire were contrasted with 325 subjects who did not return it. Those who did not return the questionnaire were slightly less educated, spent an average of twice as many years (three) unemployed, were three times as likely (11 percent) to have been in jail, twice as likely to be alcohol dependent (21 percent), and twice as likely to have IQ's under 85 (21 percent). However, those who returned questionnaires did not differ from the nonreturners, as children, in ethnicity, multiproblem family membership, emotional illness, boyhood competence, or social class. As adults they did not differ in terms of global mental health. Those who returned the Bond questionnaire did not differ significantly from those who ignored it in terms of maturity of defenses or in terms of personality disorders, but they differed dramatically in personality subtype. Men who had been rated as using reaction formation or suppression as a dominant defense were significantly more likely to return the Bond questionnaire. Men who used projection or passive aggression were significantly less likely to return it.

Our ability to predict in advance which Bond statements would correlate with which clinically assessed defense was not perfect. Nor was it as good as it would have been if Bond's statements had been relabeled in other ways—as we know with the benefit of hindsight. For example, all four of the items selected by both Vaillant's and Bond's groups to predict acting out instead identified men who, on clinical grounds, were judged to use passive aggression or dissociation. This made sense—after the fact.

However, in 50 percent or more of the cases, each of the prelabeled Bond statements was significantly correlated with the defensive style clinically identified seven years earlier (10). In other words, more than half of Bond's statements were statistically positively correlated with the clinically identified style that they were supposed to represent. On the other hand, the defensive labels assigned by Vaillant's raters seven years earlier to clinical vignettes were not just a function of context and halo effects but correlated with later self-ratings.

Bond identified five statements that he predicted would identify mature mechanisms. All were correlated with mature mechanisms at a p of $< .01$. Three correlated significantly and positively with global mental health. Bond identified 42 items intended to reflect immature defenses. If the three statements that my group could not relabel are excluded, 24 of the 39 statements were significantly and negatively correlated with maturity of defenses, and 23 were significantly correlated with clinical assessments of the specific defense that the statement was alleged to reflect. Only three of the 39 statements correlated positively with maturity of defense, none significantly; 29 of these 39 statements were also significantly and negatively correlated with global mental health.

Table 1 illustrates the significance and specificity of agreement between selected prelabeled defense statements and clinical assess-

Table 1. Specificity of Bond Questionnaire Statements

Bond Statement [Defense Label]	Strength of Correlation with Clinical Assessment of Defense Seven Years Earlier									
	Projection	Fantasy	Hypochondriasis	Passive Aggression	Dissociation	Repression	Altruism	Suppression	Sublimation	Maturity of Ego Defenses
#1. I get satisfaction from helping others and if this were taken away from me I would get depressed. [Altruism]							.21**		.18*	
#3. I'm able to keep a problem out of my mind until I have time to deal with it. [Suppression]						.24**		.26**		
#5. I work out my anxiety through doing something constructive and creative like painting or woodwork. [Sublimation]									.26**	.16*
#18. I often feel superior to people I work with. [Fantasy]		.24**								
#50. I'm shy about sex. [Isolation]		.25**								

Item								
#7. I keep getting into the same type of frustrating situations and I don't know why. [Passive aggression]	.18*	.15*	.20*		−.16*		−.23**	−.25**
#34. My friends see me as a clown. (−.12 with humor) [Passive aggression]	.18*	.31***	.15*			−.22**		−.16*
#27. I often act impulsively when something is bothering me. [Acting out]	.18*	.16*	.26*	.20**		−.21**		−.26**
#66. I am sure I get a raw deal from life. [Projection]	.20*	.26**	.31***	.21**		−.26**	−.21**	−.28**
#25. People tell me I have a persecution complex. [Projection]	.29***	.24**	.24**	.16*		−.31**	−.22**	−.24**
#53. As far as I am concerned, people are either good or bad. (−.17* with humor) [Projection/Splitting]	.25**	.22**			−.21**	−.25**	−.18**	−.24**

*p < .05; **p < .01; ***p < .001. Pearson Product Moment Correlation Coefficient.

Reprinted from Vaillant GE, Bond M, Vaillant CO. An empirically validated hierarchy of defense mechanisms. Arch Gen Psychiatry (in press). Reprinted by permission of the American Medical Association.

ment of representative defensive styles seven years previously. Statements identified as mature correlated positively with mature mechanisms but did not correlate negatively with immature mechanisms. However, some of the statements reflecting immature defensive styles consistently correlated negatively with suppression—a mature mechanism. (Suppression was the defensive style most consistently correlated with all parameters of positive mental health.) Statements associated with projection appeared to be nonspecifically correlated with other immature defenses, especially with fantasy. Perhaps because of the selective attrition of antisocial personalities, statements selected by Bond's group (e.g., #7) and by Vaillant's group (e.g., #27) to identify acting out in fact correlated more highly with dissociation (neurotic denial).

Bond's 10 lie statements were also validated. Designed to identify factitious disagreements, these 10 lie statements included six of the eight statements with which all respondents most strongly agreed; and, in sharp contrast to statements designed to assess defenses, no lie statement was significantly correlated with outcome variables.

A crude Bond scale of maturity of defenses was constructed by adding all statements prelabeled as mature and subtracting statements prelabeled projection and fantasy. This scale correlated with the global mental health score seven years earlier with an r of .48 ($p < .001$), and with maturity of defenses with an r of .35 ($p < .001$).

CONCLUSION

By contrasting two very different modes of assessing defensive style on the same sample of subjects examined seven years apart, we were able to obtain mutual support for both methods. Valid but subjective clinical judgment was contrasted with a reliable but artificial pencil and paper test. The findings suggested that clinical assessments of defensive style based on interview protocols were not just artifacts of context. They correlated significantly and specifically with self-report statements chosen to reflect that style.

Equally important, the findings supported the hypothesis that defenses reflect enduring facets of personality that are relatively stable over several years. Finally, the results also validated Bond's hypothesis that individuals have some self-awareness of their dominant defensive style.

References

1. Loevinger J: Ego Development. San Francisco, Jossey-Bass, 1976

2. Vaillant GE, Drake RE: Maturity of ego defenses in relation to *DSM-III* Axis II personality disorder. Arch Gen Psychiatry 42:597-601, 1985

3. Brenner C: Defense and defense mechanisms. Psychoanal Q 50:557-569, 1981

4. Glueck S, Glueck E: Unraveling Juvenile Delinquency. New York, The Commonwealth Fund, 1950

5. Vaillant GE: The Natural History of Alcoholism. Cambridge, MA, Harvard University Press, 1983

6. Luborsky L: Clinicians' judgments of mental health. Arch Gen Psychiatry 7:407-417, 1962

7. Vaillant GE: Theoretical hierarchy of adaptive ego mechanisms. Arch Gen Psychiatry 24:107-118, 1971

8. Vaillant GE: Natural history of male psychological health, V: the relation of choice of ego mechanisms of defense to adult adjustment. Arch Gen Psychiatry 33:535-545, 1976

9. Bond M, Gardner ST, Christian J, et al: Empirical study of self-rated defense styles. Arch Gen Psychiatry 40:333-338, 1983

10. Vaillant GE, Bond M, Vaillant CO: An empirically validated hierarchy of defense mechanisms. Arch Gen Psychiatry (in press)

6

Conceptual and Empirical Dilemmas in the Assessment of Defenses

Stuart T. Hauser, M.D., Ph.D.

6

Conceptual and Empirical Dilemmas in the Assessment of Defenses

OVERVIEW

In numerous ways, the preceding chapters highlight a major clinical research endeavor: the systematic description and measurement of defense mechanisms. As the attentive and devoted reader must by now recognize, a variety of approaches are in place for accomplishing this task. In his Introduction, Vaillant provided thoughtful observations about historical roots underlying the current efforts to assess defenses empirically, emphasizing contributions of past theoretical and empirical work. In this final chapter, I will reflect upon several key issues embedded within these current efforts, and then speculate about future directions that must now be taken.

I launch these considerations from two specific chapters (Chapters 2 and 3), which describe projects that use interview materials as the sole basis for their defense assessments. Numerous questions, implications, and research directions are sparked by these rich chapters, which convey the complexity and excitement within these projects. Depending on one's mood at the time, one can imagine this work as proceeding in a field filled either with mines, or with challenges and opportunities. Taking the opportunities-and-challenges approach, the observations that follow are organized along the lines of three *basic questions*:

1. What are defense mechanisms? Can we extract a shared conception from the work of Perry and Cooper, and of Jacobson and colleagues?
2. How can we proceed to measure these processes?
3. And assuming we can persuasively respond to the first two questions, why bother measuring these mechanisms, rather than placing our efforts on descriptive diagnostic categories and symptom assessments? Here I will cover some related domains of work, and locate the two chapters within a map of such work.

Much of this chapter will be devoted to the last and most basic of these questions, "why bother?" But we must first confront the other two questions, since they set the stage for discussing the rationale behind this ambitious enterprise.

DEFENSE MECHANISMS: CONCEPTUAL ISSUES

Both chapters view defense mechanisms as *inferred* unconscious processes—processes that mediate between the individual's impulses, wishes, and affects on the one hand, and internalized prohibitions or external reality on the other. The one exception here is "suppression," which is a partly conscious attempt to postpone, not currently confront, a particular conflict. Now it is extremely important to recognize the implications of this *core* definition. The definition does *not* imply a typology or developmental hierarchy. What is most significant is the notion of *inferred* unconscious processes. On the basis of such data as self-reported subjective states, perceptions, and sequences of action, underlying processes are inferred. Critical implications flow from this idea:

1. We cannot point to a particular behavior or statement and claim that it is the sign of an underlying defense. The behavior or speech must be seen within the context of the individual's other actions and expressions; sequence is particularly important here.

2. Our definitions of defenses must therefore specify the relevant observables—actions, expressions of meaning, and affect—together with the rules for inferring how these observed data can lead to the conclusion that a particular defense was operating. These two points must be kept clearly in focus, so that certain misunderstandings can be avoided. For example, at a recent meeting, objections were made against specific defense definitions because they described "behaviors." The energetic critic, who did not recognize the rules of inference, argued that the investigators using these definitions were mislabeling "defenses."

MEASUREMENT DILEMMAS

By holding in mind a clear view of defense mechanisms, one that can potentially be applied to empirical studies, we are prepared for our second question: How can we identify and study these constructs? I only review this area briefly, but not because I dismiss its importance. On the contrary, I think that we cannot move forward in our study of the most compelling and relevant questions, those dearest to our hearts, until we settle certain instrument difficulties. There are at least three serious problems here. The first involves the source of data. From what material are we to sample in order to measure defenses? Perry and Cooper (Chapter 2) use psychodynamic interviews and life-event vignettes. One set was videotaped; the other, I assume, audiotaped. The source for the coding in Chapter 3 is transcribed exploratory interviews—covering a set of specific topics—with patients and high school students. What degree of standardization in data collection is required so that measuring instruments can be "calibrated" to permit meaningful comparisons across studies? This first problem involves a dilemma along the following lines: A highly structured interview would insure optimal consistency across patients and studies. But such formalization might interfere with obtaining more "spontaneous" thoughts, feelings, and fantasies in the very sequences that may be most revealing of inner conflicts and the individual's defensive handling of them.

A second problem concerns the selection of defenses. Is there an agreed-upon inventory of mechanisms that can be used by investigators working in this area? Can we agree upon a "set" that is neither so narrow that it excludes clinically and theoretically important processes nor so broad that it becomes diffuse and unmanageable both for raters and for those trying to understand the results? In the Jacobson groups our specific response to this second problem has been to separately conceptualize and code ego processes that we assume may be most closely linked with highly competent behaviors although not necessarily directly related to inner conflicts.

The third problem refers to the meter or instrument itself. At this point there are at least three sets of interview-based measures: those presented by Perry and Cooper (Chapter 2); the set described by Jacobson and colleagues (Chapter 3); and the system described by Vaillant (1) in his Introduction and in Chapters 4 and 5. These systems are conceptually related, and there may be important methodological parallels as well, despite surface differences. An important next effort will be to review these similarities and differences carefully, on both conceptual and empirical levels. A fruitful outcome would be construction of a set of scales that evolve from integration of conceptual links, discovered intercorrelations, and incorporation of the most successful measurement features inherent in each of the somewhat separate scales.

RATIONALE DILEMMAS

These problems lead to demanding and consuming tasks. They involve such difficult work as recruiting (or "discovering") appropriate raters, successfully training them to achieve favorable interrater reliabilities, and developing varied strategies for grouping defenses processes. The sheer magnitude of the tasks forces us to face the final question: WHY BOTHER? In its most elaborated form, this question breaks into two more specific ones: Are these mechanisms aspects of an outmoded approach to understanding psychotherapy and its treatment? Why not use the newer and more empirically grounded diagnostic categories and criteria?

These specific questions represent important challenges that cannot be simply dismissed. A key distinction here should assist us—that of levels of complexity. A frequently used continuum ranges between molar and molecular levels. At the most molar, or macro, level are such concepts as diagnosis and stage of development (e.g., ego development) (2, 3). Then there is an intermediate level, referring to component processes or dimensions that are patterned to generate these larger categories. At the most molecular level lie more specific bits, such as discrete behaviors, attitudes, and affects. The defense mechanisms belong in the intermediate range—between such larger categories as diagnoses or stages of development on the one hand and particular affects and behaviors on the other. Using this hierarchy of complexity helps to clarify the conceptual benefits that can be gained from the study of defense processes. It also, I hope, helps us to see that "either-or" questions, or the vision of some kind of competition between diagnoses and defenses are misguided efforts.

Diagnoses and Course of Psychopathology

There are three realms of inquiry for which the systematic empirical study of defense mechanisms is highly relevant: 1) diagnosis and course of psychopathology, 2) stress and coping, 3) developmental studies. A host of meaningful questions can be conceptualized and feasibly investigated in terms of possible relations between defense mechanisms and diagnoses and psychopathology. For example, do certain patterns of defenses or shifts in defenses precede the expression of specific psychopathology, such as a major depressive episode? With respect to diagnosis, are consistent clusters of defenses associated with particular syndromes or symptom patterns? Both of these questions specifically aim toward enriching the understanding of antecedents and concomitants of diagnoses.

Another direction of work within the psychopathology realm focuses on prediction. Can certain defenses or meaningful groups of them predict later manifestations of symptoms, subsequent courses of recovery, or deterioration? This line of questioning brings us to the project that Perry and Cooper describe in Chapter 2. An important issue to be aware of here concerns base line measurement. Defenses must clearly be disentangled from symptoms. If independent measures of these constructs are taken at the time of diagnosis, and then repeated at regular intervals, investigators will be in a position to examine the possibility that these seemingly different assessments may actually be measuring the same constructs. In other words, if the symptom-defense correlation is extremely high at the time of first measurement, there is a problem of discriminant validity—that is, determining whether the same phenomenon is being measured under different labels (4). Discovering then that correlations remain high between initial defenses and later symptoms only tells us that these two remain indistinguishable. I do not think that this is the case in Perry's findings, but I raise this question so that potential fuzziness between symptoms and defenses can be diminished through both conceptual and empirical attack. A similar argument to this one can and should be made for separating defenses from psychosocial impairment—another direction taken in Perry's work.

Still another psychopathology topic has to do with consistency or constancy across situations and time. Two queries are primary here: Are some diagnoses characterized by dramatic shifts in defense usage following treatment or over the natural course of the illness? Contrariwise, in certain diagnostic groups, such as personality disorders, do the defense patterns remain stubbornly the same? These questions of consistency over time need to be distinguished from consistency across contexts. It is important to examine how specific diagnostic groups may be influenced by the present situation. Perry investigated defense usage around significant life events and the relationship of these later-assessed defenses to defense ratings completed at the time of the first interview. The strategy I am suggesting would be to attend to both 1) types of life event, and 2) aspects of psychosocial functioning. For instance, while a borderline patient may use a high degree of splitting and idealization in close relationships, these defenses might not appear in work contexts. Instead, the patient might in those situations use more isolation, intellectualization, and perhaps denial. Clinicians

are often struck by this unevenness of functioning in the successful professional or work lives of patients who seem highly impaired. The kind of analytic designs I am suggesting could lead us
to specify these "inconsistencies" more precisely and discover
vulnerability areas that are specifically linked with certain types of
psychopathology. Moreover, such studies might also help to locate
key stressors as well as competencies for these patients. This point
about variation across situations leads us to the second realm of
investigation.

Stress and Coping

This domain is an extremely popular one these days, with
thoughtful social scientists and clinical investigators in several
disciplines pursuing projects that attempt to understand how individuals adapt to (cope with) stressful circumstances (5–7). Among
the major questions are: How do aspects of the larger surroundings
(e.g., social support) and more immediate environment (e.g., family) contribute to coping? What personal resources are called upon?
Although investigators in this area attend with great vigor to
environmental characteristics, such as the nature of the stressors
and social support networks, most are equally concerned with
person dimensions—how the individual manages major acute
stresses and chronic strains. Much of the work focuses on conscious strengths—such dimensions as information-seeking, sup-
port-seeking, and modes of appraisal (8). Within the range of ways
that individuals handle stress and adapt to impossible situations
there are also more discrete strengths, such as diversity of thought,
persistence, and viewing oneself as the active agent. In our studies
(9), as I suggested earlier, we attempt to identify these dimensions
together with specific defenses. Findings from fine-grained
analyses of individuals confronting acute and chronic stresses are
likely to be a fruitful avenue toward obtaining a fuller picture of
the determinants of competence and of successful outcomes (10,
11).

One example of such a study was recently reported by Snarey
and Vaillant (12), who studied the question of how working-class

youth become middle-class adults—how they defy the odds and become exceptions to the "rule," supported by repeated observations that children's social class is a stubborn predictor of their adult social class standing. Through a series of careful interview codings and multivariate analyses, Snarey and Vaillant found that three defense mechanisms, scored from adult interviews, accounted for a significant degree of variance in upward social mobility. Intellectualization, altruism, and anticipation, the three defenses, were highly correlated with upward mobility even after intelligence, boyhood ego strengths, and parent education were taken into account. I cannot possibly do justice to this most interesting study, but I cite it as an excellent example of how investigating defenses—and other adaptive strengths—can contribute to an understanding of the precursors and nature of resilience, the other side of psychopathology.

Developmental Studies

The relationship of defenses to lines of childhood, adolescent, and adult development is relatively uncharted territory. Vaillant's *Adapation to Life* (1) represents one important series of studies directed to this question. In a more speculative fashion, Anna Freud considered this topic in at least two works (13, 14). Large questions remain to be explored: How do earlier defense processes covary with changes in developmental stages, such as those of psychosexual ego and cognitive development? More specifically, does the use of particular defenses by an adolescent require certain levels of cognitive or ego development? To what extent do developmental advances depend upon, require, the availability of particular defense mechanisms and other personal resources? The work of our group (15, 16), discussed in Chapter 3, is revelant to these lines of inquiry. Through The Adolescent and Family Development project, we are investigating the linkages, possibly causal relationships, between defense patterns and variations in adolescent ego development (2). The striking correlations between ego development and specific defenses that are discussed in Chapter 3 are contributions toward this goal. The findings and instruments described in another recent paper from our project (9) concern other ego processes relevant to adaptation. Ultimately, it is hoped that this kind of longitudinal work will help to delineate the role of defenses in specific types of development and will contribute empirically to a more accurate conceptualization of a developmental typology of defenses. With respect to this last point, we are specifically not collapsing the defenses into "mature," "intermediate," and "immature" groupings. Instead, we are leaving the issue open, to be studied through the developmental evidence itself.

I hope that in reviewing the relevance of defense studies to psychopathology, stress and coping, and developmental investigations, I have been able to convey the potential harvest that can be gathered through arduous and ambitious empirical enterprises. It is a credit to these chapters that so rich an array of possibilities can be brought foward.

References

1. Vaillant G: Adaptation to Life. Boston, Little, Brown, 1977

2. Loevinger J: Ego Development. San Francisco, Jossey-Bass, 1976

3. Hauser S: Loevinger's model and measure of ego development: a critical review. Psychol Bul 83:928-958, 1976

4. Campbell D, Fiske D: Convergent and discriminate validation by the multi-trait, multi-method matrix. Psychol Bul 56:81-105, 1959

5. Goldberger L, Breznitz S: Handbook of Stress. New York, Free Press, 1982

6. Dohrenwend BS, Krasnoff L, Askenasy A, et al: The Psychiatric Epidemiology Research Interview Life Events Scale, in Handbook of Stress. Edited by Goldberger L, Breznitz S. New York, Free Press, 1982

7. Billings A, Cronkite R, Moos R: Social–environmental factors in unipolar depression: comparisons of depressed patients and non-depressed controls. J Abnorm Psychol 92:119-133, 1983

8. Lazarus R, Folkman S: Stress, Appraisal, and Coping. New York, Springer, 1984

9. Beardslee W, Jacobson A, Hauser S, et al: An approach to evaluating adolescent adaptive processes: scale development and reliability. J Am Acad Child Psychiatry 24:637-642, 1985

10. Garmezy N: The study of competence in children at risk for psychopathology, in The Child in His Family: Children at Psychiatric Risk. Edited by Anthonty EJ, Koupernik C. New York, Wiley, 1974

11. Hauser S, Vieyra M, Jacobson A, et al: Vulnerability and resiliency in adolescence: views from the family. J Early Adolescence 5:81-100, 1985

12. Snarey JR, Vaillant GE: How lower and working-class youth become middle-class adults: the association between ego defense mechanisms and upward mobility. Child Dev 56:889-910, 1985

13. Freud A: The Ego and the Mechanisms of Defense (1937). New York, International Universities Press, 1966

14. Freud A: Normality and Pathology in Childhood. New York, International Universities Press, 1965

15. Hauser S, Jacobson A, Noam G, et al: Ego development and self-image complexity in early adolescence. Arch Gen Psychiatry 40:325-331, 1983

16. Jacobson AM, Hauser ST, Powers S, et al: The influences of chronic illness and ego development on self-esteem in diabetic and psychiatric adolescent patients. J Youth and Adolescence 13:489-507, 1985

Appendix:
Six Assessment Schemes for
Defense Mechanisms

Index to Comparative Glossary Definitions of Defenses Defined by More Than One Author*

	Glossary				
	I DSM-III (R)	II CTP/III	III Vaillant	IV Perry	V Hauser et al.
Acting out	X	X	X	X	X
Altruism	X	X	X	X	X
Anticipation		X	X	X	
Asceticism		X			X
Denial	X	X	X		X
Devaluation	X			X	
Displacement	X	X	X	X	X
Dissociation	X	X	X	X	
Distortion		X	X		
Fantasy	X	X	X	X	
Humor	X	X	X	X	
Hypochondriasis		X	X	X	
Idealization	X			X	
Intellectualization	X	X	X	X	X
Isolation	X	X		X	
Passive aggression (turning against the self)	X	X	X	X	X
Projection	X	X	X	X	X
Projection (delusional)		X	X		
Rationalization	X	X		X	X
Reaction formation	X	X	X	X	
Regression	X	X			
Repression	X	X	X	X	X
Somatization	X	X			
Splitting	X			X	
Sublimation	X	X	X	X	
Suppression	X	X	X	X	X
Undoing	X			X	

* The defenses "Blocking," "Controlling," "Externalization," "Introjection," "Inhibition," and "Sexualization" are defined only in the *Comprehensive Textbook of Psychiatry* (Appendix, part II).

The defenses "Bland denial," "Projective identification," "Omnipotence," "Neurotic denial," "Affiliation," "Self-observation," and "Self-assertion," are defined only by Perry (Appendix, part IV).

The defense "Avoidance" is defined only by Hauser (Appendix, part V).

I. A Draft Glossary of Defense Mechanisms for *DSM-III* (R)[1]

DEFENSE MECHANISMS

Patterned feelings, thoughts, or behaviors that are relatively involuntary and arise in response to perceptions of psychic dangers. They are designed to hide or alleviate the conflicts or stresses that give rise to the anxiety signal. Some of these defense mechanisms, such as projection, splitting, and acting out, are almost invariably maladaptive. Others, such as suppression and denial, may be either maladaptive or adaptive depending on their severity, their inflexibility, and the context in which they occur. Still others, such as sublimation and humor, are usually adaptive.

1. *Acting out:* The individual deals with emotional conflicts, or internal or external stressors, by acting without reflection or apparent regard for negative consequences.
2. *Altruism:* The individual deals with emotional conflicts, or internal or external stressors, by dedication to fulfilling the needs of others, in part as a way of fulfilling his or her own needs.
3. *Autistic fantasy:* The individual deals with emotional conflicts, or internal or external stressors, by excessive daydreaming as a substitute for human relationships, more direct and effective action, or problem solving.

[1]This glossary is the result of the work of the Advisory Committee on Defense Mechanisms—Dr. David Barlow, Dr. Michael Bond, Dr. Allen Frances, Dr. William Frosch, Dr. J. Christopher Perry, Dr. George Vaillant, Dr. Jeff Young, and Dr. Robert Spitzer, Chairman, Work Group to Revise *DSM-III*. The glossary has not yet been approved by the American Psychiatric Association and is subject to revision at any time. Copyright by the American Psychiatric Association. Reprinted by permission.

4. *Denial:* The individual deals with emotional conflicts, or internal or external stressors, by refusing to acknowledge some aspect of external reality that would be apparent to others.

5. *Devaluation:* The individual deals with emotional conflicts, or internal or external stressors, by attributing exaggerated negative qualities to self or others.

6. *Displacement:* The individual deals with emotional conflicts, or internal or external stressors, by generalizing or redirecting a feeling about or a response to an object onto another, usually less threatening, object.

7. *Dissociation:* The individual deals with emotional conflicts, or internal or external stressors, by a temporary alteration in the integrative functions of consciousness or identity.

8. *Humor:* The individual deals with emotional conflicts, or internal or external stressors, by emphasizing the amusing or ironic aspects of the conflict or stressor.

9. *Idealization:* The individual deals with emotional conflicts, or internal or external stressors, by attributing exaggerated positive qualities to self or others.

10. *Intellectualization:* The individual deals with emotional conflicts, or internal or external stressors, by the excessive use of abstract thinking to avoid experiencing disturbing feelings.

11. *Isolation:* The individual deals with emotional conflicts, or internal or external stressors, by being unable to experience simultaneously the cognitive and affective components of an experience, because the affect is kept from consciousness.

12. *Passive aggression:* The individual deals with emotional conflicts, or internal or external stressors, by indirectly and unassertively expressing aggression toward others.

13. *Projection:* The individual deals with emotional conflicts, or internal or external stressors, by falsely attributing his or her own unacknowledged feelings, impulses, or thoughts to others.

14. *Rationalization:* The individual deals with emotional conflicts, or internal or external stressors, by devising reassuring

or self-serving but incorrect explanations for his or her own or others' behavior.

15. *Reaction formation:* The individual deals with emotional conflicts, or internal or external stressors, by substituting behavior, thoughts, or feelings that are diametrically opposed to his or her unacceptable thoughts or feelings.

16. *Repression:* The individual deals with emotional conflicts, or internal or external stressors, by being unable to remember or be cognitively aware of disturbing wishes, feelings, thoughts, or experiences.

17. *Somatization:* The individual deals with emotional conflicts, or internal or external stressors, by preoccupation with physical symptoms disproportionate to any actual physical disturbance.

18. *Splitting:* The individual deals with emotional conflicts, or internal or external stressors, by viewing himself or herself or others as all good or all bad, failing to integrate the positive and negative qualities of self and others into cohesive images; often the same individual will be alternately idealized and devalued.

19. *Sublimation:* The individual deals with emotional conflicts, or internal or external stressors, by channeling personally unacceptable feelings or impulses into socially desirable behavior.

20. *Suppression:* The individual deals with emotional conflicts, or internal or external stressors, by intentionally avoiding thinking about disturbing problems, wishes, feelings, or experiences.

21. *Undoing:* The individual deals with emotional conflicts, or internal or external stressors, by behavior designed to symbolically make amends for or negate previous thoughts, feelings, or actions.

II. Glossary of Defenses from *Modern Synopsis of Comprehensive Textbook of Psychiatry/III.*[1]

A. NARCISSISTIC DEFENSES

Denial: psychotic denial of external reality. Unlike repression, it affects the perception of external reality more than the perception of internal reality. Seeing but refusing to acknowledge what one sees and hearing but negating what is actually heard are examples of denial and exemplify the close relationship of denial to sensory experience. However, not all denial is necessarily psychotic. Like projection, denial may function in the service of neurotic or even adaptive objectives.

Distortion: grossly reshaping external reality to suit inner needs— including unrealistic megalomanic beliefs, hallucinations, and wish-fulfilling delusions—and using sustained feelings of delusional superiority or entitlement.

Projection: frank delusions about external reality, usually persecutory; it includes both perception of one's own feelings in another and subsequent acting on the perception (psychotic paranoid delusions).

B. IMMATURE DEFENSES

Acting out: direct expression of an unconscious wish or impulse to avoid being conscious of the accompanying affect. The unconscious fantasy, involving objects, is lived out impulsively in behavior, thus gratifying the impulse more than the prohibition

---

[1]Reprinted from Kaplan HI, Sadock BJ: Modern Synopsis of Comprehensive Textbook of Psychiatry/III, pp. 137–138. Baltimore, Williams & Wilkins, 1981. Reprinted by permission.

against it. On a chronic level, acting out involves giving in to impulses to avoid the tension that would result from postponement of expression.

Blocking: inhibition, usually temporary in nature, of affects (usually), thinking, or impulses.

Hypochondriasis: transformation of reproach toward others—arising from bereavement, loneliness, or unacceptable aggressive impulses—into self-reproach and complaints of pain, somatic illness, and neurasthenia. Existent illness may also be overemphasized or exaggerated for its evasive and regressive possibilities. Thus, responsibility may be avoided, guilt may be circumvented, and instinctual impulses may be warded off.

Introjection: with a loved object, introjection involves the internalization of characteristics of the object with the goal of establishing closeness to and constant presence of the object. Anxiety consequent to separation or tension arising out of ambivalence toward the object is thus diminished. Introjection of a feared object serves to avoid anxiety by internalizing the aggressive characteristics of the object, thereby putting the aggression under one's own control. The aggression is no longer felt as coming from outside but is taken within and used defensively, turning the person's weak, passive position into an active, strong one. Introjection can also rise out of a sense of guilt, in which the self-punishing introject is attributable to the hostile-destructive component of an ambivalent tie to an object. The self-punitive qualities of the object are taken over and established within one's self as a symptom or character trait, which effectively represents both the destruction and the preservation of the object. This is also called identification with the victim.

Passive-aggressive behavior: aggression toward an object expressed indirectly and ineffectively through passivity, masochism, and turning against the self.

Projection: attributing one's own unacknowledged feelings to others; it includes severe prejudice, rejection of intimacy through suspiciousness, hypervigilance to external danger, and injustice collecting. Projection operates correlatively to introjection; the material of the projection is derived from the internalized configuration of the introjects.

Regression: return to a previous state of development or functioning to avoid the anxieties or hostilities involved in later stages; return to earlier points of fixation, embodying modes of behavior previously given up. This defense mechanism is often the result of a disruption of equilibrium at a later phase of development.

Schizoid fantasy: tendency to use fantasy and to indulge in autistic retreat for the purpose of conflict resolution and gratification.

Somatization: defensive conversion of psychic derivatives into bodily symptoms.

C. NEUROTIC DEFENSES

Controlling: excessive attempt to manage or regulate events or objects in the environment in the interest of minimizing anxiety and solving internal conflicts.

Displacement: purposeful, unconscious shifting from one object to another in the interest of solving a conflict. Although the object is changed, the instinctual nature of the impulse and its aim remain unchanged.

Dissociation: temporary but drastic modification of character or sense of personal identity to avoid emotional distress; it involves fugue states and hysterical conversion reactions.

Externalization: tendency to perceive in the external world and in external objects components of one's own personality, including instinctual impulses, conflicts, moods, attitudes, and styles of thinking. It is a more general term than projection, which is defined by its derivation from and correlation with specific introjects.

Inhibition: unconsciously determined limitation or renunciation of specific ego functions, singly or in combination, to avoid anxiety arising out of conflict with instinctual impulses, the superego, or environmental forces or figures.

Intellectualization: control of affects and impulses by thinking about them instead of experiencing them. It is a systematic excess of thinking, deprived of its affect, to defend against anxiety due to unacceptable impulses.

Isolation: intrapsychic splitting or separation of affect from content, resulting in repression of either idea or affect or the displacement of affect to a different or substitute content.

Rationalization: justification of attitudes, beliefs, or behavior that may otherwise be unacceptable by an incorrect application of justifying reasons or the invention of a convincing fallacy.

Reaction formation: management of unacceptable impulses by permitting expression of the impulse in antithetical form.

Repression: expelling and withholding from conscious awareness of an idea or feeling. It may operate by excluding from awareness what was once experienced on a conscious level (secondary repression), or it may curb ideas and feelings before they have reached consciousness (primary repression). The "forgetting" of repression is unique in that it is often accompanied by highly symbolic behavior, which suggests that the repressed is not really forgotten.

Sexualization: endowing of an object or function with sexual significance that it did not previously have or that it possesses to a lesser degree to ward off anxieties connected with prohibited impulses.

Somatization: defensive conversion of psychic derivatives into bodily symptoms.

D. MATURE DEFENSES

Altruism: vicarious but constructive and instinctually gratifying service to others. This defense mechanism must be distinguished from altruistic surrender, which involves a surrender of direct gratification or of instinctual needs in favor of fulfilling the needs of others to the detriment of the self, with vicarious satisfaction being gained only through introjection.

Anticipation: realistic anticipation of or planning for future inner discomfort.

Asceticism: elimination of directly pleasurable affects attributable to an experience. The moral element is implicit in setting values on specific pleasures. Asceticism is directed against all base pleasures perceived consciously; gratification is derived from the renunciation.

Humor: overt expression of feelings without personal discomfort or immobilization and without unpleasant effect on others. Humor allows one to bear and yet focus on what is too terrible to be borne; in contrast, wit involves distraction or displacement away from the affective issue.

Sublimation: gratification of an impulse whose goal is retained but whose aim or object is changed from a socially objectionable one to a socially valued one. Libidinal sublimation involves a desexualization of drive impulses and the placing of a value judgment that substitutes what is valued by the superego or society. Sublimation of aggressive impulses takes place through pleasurable games and sports. Unlike neurotic defenses, sublimation allows instincts to be channeled, rather than dammed or diverted. In sublimation, feelings are acknowledged, modified, and directed toward a relatively significant person or goal, so that modest instinctual satisfaction results.

Suppression: conscious or semiconscious decision to postpone attention to a conscious impulse or conflict.

III. Vaillant's Glossary of Defenses[1]

A. "PSYCHOTIC" DEFENSES

These mechanisms are common in "healthy" individuals before age five, and common in adult dreams and fantasy. For the *user*, these mechanisms alter reality. To the *beholder*, they appear "crazy." They tend to be immune to change by conventional psychotherapeutic interpretation; but they are *altered* by change in reality (e.g., chlorpromazine, removal of stressful situation, developmental maturation). In therapy they can be given up temporarily by offering the user strong interpersonal support in conjunction with direct confrontation with the ignored reality.

1. *Delusional projection:* frank delusions about external reality, usually of a persecutory type.

   It includes both the perception of one's own feelings in another person and then acting on the perception (e.g., florid paranoid delusions), and the perception of other people or their feelings literally inside one's self (e.g., the agitated depressed patient's claim that "the devil is devouring my heart"). This mechanism can be distinguished from *projection* by the fact that in *delusional projection*, reality testing is virtually abandoned. It is distinguished from distortion by the absence of wish fulfillment and from introjection in that the responsibility for acknowledged internal feelings is still projected. In toxic psychosis, *delusional projection* can adaptively organize otherwise chaotic perceptions.

---

[1]For justification of definitions, see Table 1 in Vaillant GE: Theoretical hierarchy of adaptive ego mechanisms. Arch Gen Psychiatry 24:107–118, 1971.

2. *Denial (psychotic):* denial of external reality.

Unlike repression, *denial*, as here defined, affects perception of external reality more than perception of internal reality (for example, "girls do so got penises"). It includes the use
of fantasy as a major substitute for other people—especially
absent other people (e.g., "I will make a new him in my own
mind").

3. *Distortion:* grossly reshaping external reality to suit inner
needs.

It includes unrealistic megalomaniacal beliefs: hallucinations, wish-fulfilling delusions, and employing sustained feelings of delusional superiority or entitlement. It can encompass
persistent denial of personal responsibility for one's own behavior. It also includes acting upon, as well as thinking about,
unrealistic obsessions or compulsions. In distortion, there may
be a pleasant merging or fusion with another person (e.g.,
"Jesus lives inside me and answers all my prayers"); but in
contrast to *delusional projection*, where distress is alleviated
by assigning responsibility for offensive feelings elsewhere, in
distortion unpleasant feelings are replaced with their opposites. As manifested in religious belief, *distortion* can be
highly adaptive.

B. "IMMATURE" DEFENSES

These mechanisms are common in "healthy" individuals age
three to 15, in character disorder, and in adults in psychotherapy.
For the *user* these mechanisms most often alter distress engen-
dered either by the threat of interpersonal intimacy or the threat
of experiencing its loss. To the *beholder* they appear socially unde-
sirable. Although refractory to change, they change with improved interpersonal relationships (e.g., personal maturation, a
more mature spouse, a more intuitive physician, or a fairer parole
officer) or with repeated and forceful interpretation during prolonged psychotherapy.

4. *Projection:* attributing one's own unacknowledged feelings to
others.

It includes severe prejudice, rejections of intimacy through unwarranted suspicion, marked hypervigilance to external danger, and injustice collecting. The behavior of someone using this defense may be eccentric and abrasive but within the "letter of the law." It includes much "devaluation."

5. *Schizoid fantasy:* tendency to use fantasy, autistic retreat, and imaginary relationships for the purpose of conflict resolution and gratification.

It is associated with global avoidance of interpersonal intimacy and the use of eccentricity to repel others. In contrast to psychotic *denial*, the individual does not fully believe in or insist upon acting out his fantasies. Nevertheless, unlike mere wishes, schizoid fantasies serve to gratify unmet needs for personal relationships, and to obliterate the overt expression of aggressive or sexual impulses toward others. It includes much "primitive idealization."

6. *Hypochondriasis:* the transformation of reproach toward others arising from bereavement, loneliness, or unacceptable aggressive impulses into first self-reproach and then complaints of pain, somatic illness, and neurasthenia.

It includes those aspects of introjection which permit traits of an ambivalently regarded person to be perceived within oneself and causing plausible disease. Unlike identification, hypochondriacal introjects are "ego alien." The mechanism may permit the individual to belabor others with his own pain or discomfort in lieu of making direct demands upon them or in lieu of complaining that others have ignored his wishes (often unexpressed) to be dependent. It does *not* include illnesses like asthma, ulcer, or hypertension, which may be neither adaptive nor defensive. Unlike hysterical conversion symptoms, hypochondriasis is accompanied by the very opposite of *la belle indifference.*

7. *Passive-aggressive behavior:* aggression toward others expressed indirectly and ineffectively through passivity.

It includes failures, procrastinations, or illnesses that (initially at least) affect others more than self. It includes silly or provocative behavior in order to receive attention, and clowning in order to avoid assuming a competitive role. People who form sadomasochistic relationships often manifest both *passive-aggressive* and *hypochondriacal* defenses.

8. *Acting out:* direct expression of an unconscious wish or impulse in order to avoid being conscious of the affect or the ideation that accompanies it.

   It includes the use of motor behavior, delinquent or impulsive acts, and "tempers" to avoid being aware of one's feelings. It also includes the chronic use of drugs, failure, perversion, or self-inflicted injury to relieve tension (i.e., subjective anxiety or depression). Acting out involves chronically giving in to impulses in order to avoid the tension that would result were there any postponement of expression.

9. *Dissociation:* temporary but drastic modification of one's character or of one's sense of personal identity to avoid emotional distress.

   This can include fugues, most hysterical conversion reactions, a sudden unwarranted sense of superiority or devil-may-care attitude and *short-term* refusal to perceive responsibility for one's acts or feelings. It also includes overactivity and counterphobic behavior to blot out anxiety or distressing emotion, "safe" expression of instinctual wishes through acting on stage, and the *acute* use of religious "joy" or of pharmacological intoxication to numb unhappiness. *Dissociation* is more comprehensible to others than *distortion*, more considerate of others and less prolonged than *acting out*. It is synonymous with neurotic denial and perhaps with "omnipotence."

"NEUROTIC" DEFENSES

These mechanisms are common in "healthy" individuals age three through 90, in neurotic disorder, and in mastering acute adult stress. For the *user* these mechanisms alter private feelings or instinctual expression. To the *beholder*, they appear as individual quirks or neurotic hang-ups. They often can be dramatically *changed* by conventional, brief psychotherapeutic interpretation.

10. *Repression:* seemingly inexplicable naiveté, memory lapse, or

failure to acknowledge input from a selected sense organ. In *isolation*, the idea is kept in mind and the affect forgotten; in *repression*, the idea is repressed and the affect often remains. The "forgetting" of repression is unique in that it is often accompanied by highly symbolic behavior which suggests that the repressed is *not really* forgotten. The mechanism differs from *suppression* by effecting unconscious inhibition of impulse to the point of losing, not just postponing, cherished goals. Unlike *denial*, it prevents the expression and perception of instincts and feelings rather than affecting recognition of and response to external events. If a man were weeping but forgot for whom he wept, this would be *repression*; if he denied the existence of his tears or insisted that the mourned one was still alive, this would represent *denial*; if he denied that he felt sad, that would be *dissociation*.

11. *Displacement:* the redirection of feelings toward a relatively less cared-for (less cathected) object than the person or situation arousing the feelings.

    It includes facile "transference" and the substitution of things or strangers for emotionally important people. Practical jokes, with hidden hostile intent, and caricature involve displacement. Most phobias, a few hysterical conversion reactions, and some prejudice involve displacement.

12. *Reaction formation:* conscious affect and/or behavior that is diametrically opposed to an unacceptable instinctual (id) impulse.

    This mechanism includes overtly caring for someone else when one wishes to be cared for oneself, "hating" someone or something one really likes, or "loving" a hated rival or unpleasant duty. The term can encompass both "identification with the aggressor" and "altruism" as defined by Anna Freud.

13. *Intellectualization:* thinking about instinctual wishes in formal, bland terms that leave the associated affect unconscious.

    The term encompasses the mechanisms of isolation, rationalization, ritual, undoing, restitution, magical thinking, and "busy work." While these mechanisms differ from each other, they usually occur as a cluster. Intellectualization includes paying undue attention to the inanimate in order to avoid intimacy with people, or paying attention to external reality to avoid recognition of inner feelings, or paying attention to irrelevant detail to avoid perceiving the whole. Obsessions and compulsions not acted upon are included here, although they can also be thought of as a form of intrapsychic *displacement*.

D. "MATURE" DEFENSES

These mechanisms are common in "healthy" individuals aged 12 to 90. For the *user* these mechanisms integrate reality, interpersonal relationships, and private feelings. To the *beholder*, they appear as convenient virtues. Under increased stress they may *change* to less mature mechanisms.

14. *Altruism:* vicarious but constructive and instinctually gratifying service to others.

    It can include benign and constructive reaction formation, empathy, philanthropy, and well-repaid service to others. Altruism differs from *projection* in that it responds to needs of others that are real and not projected; it differs from *reaction formation* in that it leaves the person at least partly gratified when he is doing for others as he wishes to be done by.

15. *Humor:* overt expression of feelings without individual discomfort or immobilization and without unpleasant effect on others.

    Some games and playful regression come under this heading. Unlike wit, which is a form of *displacement*, humor lets you call a spade a spade; and *humor* can never be applied without some element of an "observing ego." Like hope, *humor* permits one to bear and yet focus upon what is too terrible to be borne; in contrast, wit always involves distraction or displacement away from the affective issue at hand. Unlike *schizoid fantasy, humor* never excludes other people.

16. *Suppression:* the capacity to hold all components of a conflict in mind and then to postpone action, affective response, or ideational worrying.

Suppression appears as a semiconscious decision to defer
paying attention to a conscious impulse or conflict. The
mechanism includes looking for silver linings, stoicism, minimizing acknowledged discomfort, employing a stiff upper lip,
and "counting to 10" before acting. With *suppression*, one
says, "I will think about it tomorrow," and the next day one
remembers to think about it. With *repression*, one forgets to
remember.

17. *Anticipation:* realistic anticipation of or planning for future
inner discomfort.

This mechanism includes goal-directed but overly careful
affective planning or worrying, anticipatory mourning and
anxiety, and the conscious utilization of "insight" gained
from psychotherapy.

18. *Sublimation:* indirect or attenuated expression of instincts
without adverse consequences or marked loss of pleasure.

It includes both expression of aggression through pleasurable games, sports, and hobbies, and romantic attenuation of
instinctual expression during a real courtship. Unlike humor,
with *sublimation* "regression in the service of the ego" has
real consequences. Unlike the case with "neurotic defenses,"
with *sublimation* instincts are channeled rather than
dammed or diverted. In *projection* one's feelings (e.g., anger)
are attributed to another person. In *displacement* one's feelings are acknowledged as one's own, but are redirected toward
a relatively insignificant object, often without satisfaction. In
sublimation feelings are acknowledged, modified, and directed toward a relatively significant person or goal so that
modest instinctual satisfaction results.

CASE ILLUSTRATIONS

A woman, married at age 30, had one miscarriage and then tried
for seven years to have children. Then, following a cervical biopsy
that showed early cancer, at age 38 she underwent a total hysterectomy. She had always felt inadequate to her younger sister, who
already had four children and had been the one in the family who

won praise as "being good with kids." The woman's husband desperately wanted children. (Note that the conflict involves instinctual wishes, parental expectations, reality, and the needs of those she loved.) Below are a number of possible responses to her surgery:

A. A month after surgery, the woman organized a group of other women who had had breast and uterine surgery to counsel and visit patients undergoing gynecological surgery. They tried to give information, advice, and comfort and from their experience to provide answers to questions and fears that such new patients might have. [Altruism]

B. Following a slight postoperative wound infection, she wrote long, angry letters to the papers blaming the hospital for unsanitary conditions. Blaming her doctor for not doing a Pap smear earlier, she threatened to institute malpractice proceedings. [Projection]

C. She renewed her old college interest in planned parenthood and passionately argued with her younger friends to limit their families. She suddenly "remembered" that she had always been afraid of the pain of childbirth and remarked to her husband how lucky she was to be spared the burden. [Reaction formation]

D. She read a lot about uterine cancer and asked the doctor a great many questions about the nature of the operation. She concerned herself with minute details of preventing postoperative infection and caring for her operative wound. She made a hobby in the hospital of learning medical words. [Isolation]

E. Emerging from anesthesia she felt no regret but instead enjoyed what she felt was a religious experience. Postoperatively, she told all her friends that her pain gave her a sense of joyous communion with sufferers everywhere. She felt an intense inward sense of good fortune that she had been favored by God to have had her cancer discovered so soon and to have come through surgery so well. [Dissociation]

F. She read Marcus Aurelius and Ecclesiastes in the hospital. She took great care to hide her tear-stained facial tissues from her husband and made no complaint (even though the process was painful) while her sutures were removed. Knowing that baby pictures upset her, she deliberately gave away an unread copy of her favorite magazine, which featured an article on child care. [Suppression]

G. She found herself unable to remember the name of the operation, except that it was for "a little nubbin in my tum-tum." She "forgot" her first follow-up visit to the physician. On coming home she broke into tears when she broke an inexpensive, amphora-shaped flower vase; she had no idea why. [Repression]

H. She started ordering the nurses to move her upstairs to the maternity ward. She wandered about the hospital looking for *her* baby. She experienced no postoperative pain. [Denial]

I. She got great pleasure from "get well" cards from her sister's children, agreed to teach a Sunday School class of preschoolers, and had a poem published in her hometown weekly on the bittersweet joys of the maiden aunt. [Sublimation]

J. She became very interested in growing tulips and daffodils in her hospital window. Although she never asked the doctor questions about her own hospital course, she worried about a funny mold on the bulbs she was growing. Knowing his hobby was gardening, she repeatedly asked her surgeon's advice about the growth on her bulbs. [Displacement]

K. On the third postoperative day she announced that she was signing out immediately. Besides, she had to go home because she and her husband were planning a trip to Bermuda that weekend. (In reality, their total income was $200 a week and their Blue Cross insurance had lapsed.) She added with a naughty laugh that they needed a vacation to do a little "spring planting." [Distortion]

L. Her doctor was surprised to find out how relaxed and practical she was about her postoperative course and the calm frankness with which she could express her regret at being cheated of children. He was surprised because she had spent her preoperative visit anxiously worrying about possible surgical complications and weeping over the fact that she would never be able to bear children. [Anticipation]

M. She felt that the hospital was being run by racists who were trying to sterilize her. She tried to telephone the FBI to report the hospital for genocide. She refused her pain medication, claiming it was an experimental drug for thought control. [Delusional projection]

N. She asked the nurse not to permit visitors because they made her "sad." She threw out all her flowers and instead read and reread a copy of *Parents* magazine and *The Family of Man*. She would go down the corridor to the newborn nursery daydreaming about what she would call each child if it were hers, and once a floor nurse had to ask her not to whistle lullabys so loudly. [Fantasy]

O. She became worried that the cancer might have spread to her lymph nodes and belabored her visitors with accounts of the tiny lumps in her groin and neck. When her sister came to visit, she angrily accused her of caring so much for her own children that she did not care if her own sister died of cancer. [Hypochondriasis]

P. When the intern, while inserting an IV, missed her vein, she smiled at him, told him not to worry, and said, "When you're *just* a medical student, it must be hard to get things right." Unable to sleep, she watched her IV run dry. Later, at 4 AM, the night nurse had to call the intern to restart the IV. She cheerfully told him that she had not rung for the nurse because she knew how busy everyone in the hospital was. [Passive aggression]

Q. Shortly after leaving the hospital she was unfaithful to her husband with four different men in a month, twice picking up men in cocktail lounges and once seducing an 18-year-old delivery boy. Prior to that time she had had no sexual interest in any man but her husband. [Acting out]

R. She laughed so hard tears came to her eyes and her ribs ached when she read the *Playboy* definition of a hysterectomy, "throwing out the baby carriage but keeping the playpen." She explained her private mirth to a startled and curious nurse with, "The whole thing is just so damned ironic." [Humor]

IV. Perry's Clinical Defense Mechanism Rating Scales, and Glossary of Defenses

INTRODUCTION AND DIRECTIONS

The following scales are designed for use in making reliable judgments of the probability that a given subject uses each of the defense mechanisms represented. A psychodynamically oriented clinical interview of the subject serves as the source upon which the rater or raters base their ratings. The interviewer himself is thus not a direct clinical source of ratings of defense mechanisms. Rather, the recent history offered by the subject, relevant life vignettes, and the interaction between the subject and the interviewer serve as the data base from which the observer-raters make their ratings of defense mechanisms. While removing the interviewer from the role of rater may sacrifice some of the subjective and valuable perceptions about what effect the subject was having upon the interviewer, there is a gain in greater objectivity. This is highly desirable from the point of view of research.

The scales are representations of the concept defining each defense mechanism. If an attempt were made to rate a subject's interview using the definitions alone, however, very few ratings would be reliable. This has been the problem with psychodynamic concepts and research in general. To facilitate reliable application of each definition, the scales were designed with the scores of probable and definite use anchored by examples or further observation rules. The best application of the scales requires a continual process of checking back and forth between the idea behind the scale (i.e., the defenses's definition) and the scale anchorings. It requires judgment, which will be an inevitable source of error as well.

Ratings can be made in two ways, by individual observers or by groups of observers. In either case it is best if the subject's interview is videotaped, and the videotape is played to the observer-raters. This is for ease in administration. It also eliminates a possible source of subject distraction (which would be an unwanted source of variance) by removing the raters from the subject's sight.

After the interview has been observed, each rater reads through each scale one at a time. He makes a rating of the probability that the subject employs the respective defense (rated on a 0 to 2 scale representing not probable, probable, and definite use of the defense). The answers are recorded on the summary answer sheet before the rater is allowed to discuss his ratings with other raters. This blind method enhances each rater's learning as well as protects each rater from being biased by others' ratings.

If raters are being trained, or if a group consensus rating is desired, then one further step is added. The raters (an expert rater, if the purpose is training the novice raters) discuss their respective ratings of each defense mechanism one by one. The purpose is to develop a consensual rating, which is more accurate than taking the mean of what all the raters' scores would be. Here the process of developing the consensus is important.

The person with the highest rating offers the evidence from the interview and makes the case for his rating. The raters in the group are the final arbiters of what they did or did not observe in the interview. The individual defenses' definitions and scales are the guide to forming a rating once the data from the interview are defined and accepted. This two-step process (first agree on the relevant data, then agree on the rating) is designed to maximize subject variance and minimize interrater (or consensual group) variance and prevent regression to the mean for all subjects on all scales.

RESTRICTIONS IN INTERPRETING RELEVANT INTERVIEW DATA

Psychodynamic structures are not static but change with time, while one's history grows in accretions leaving the past unchanged. It would be a mistake, for instance, to rate a subject as using a particular defense based on a historical event reported from 20 years ago. This would make the scales insensitive to change. Certain restrictions are therefore necessary to delimit the data one heeds in making ratings.

1. To give a rating of 2 on a given defense scale, there must be some clear evidence from a period of time within two years of the present interview of the subject.

2. A clear example of the use of a defense based on evidence older than two years may itself not be used to give a 2 rating. It may, however, influence the interpretation of otherwise difficult data from the more recent two-year period. Thus, the past example can be used to focus the present data more clearly but not as a substitute for it.

3. As a rule, the more examples the subject gives, and the more recently they occurred, the more they count in raising the subject's score on the relevant defense. Evidence from interaction within the interview itself is particularly relevant in this regard.

4. The same data can be evidence for use of one or two, but not more than two defenses. This is particularly true for some "nearest neighbor" defenses such as hypochondriasis and passive aggression, where an example may appear to fall between the two definitions. In fact, both defenses may be used. With some defenses, however, clear rules have been offered to minimize confusion between defenses. This is desirable to limit confounding one defense with another.

5. The scales are intended to rate defenses that are characteristic of a subject. In those cases in which a subject has an episodic disorder, such as bipolar mania or schizophrenia, one should consider examples as less important in contributing to any defense rating, if they probably or definitely occurred during an episode of that disorder than if they occurred between symptomatic episodes. Such a distinction is sometimes difficult to make.

An Example of Defense Rating Scale:

Neurotic Denial (Minor Denial)

Scoring Method:

0: No examples present.

1: Probable use of denial.
   a. The subject describes a life situation where one would think that certain feelings like anger, sadness, or fear might be present, but the subject denies that they were (are).
   b. The subject denies certain feelings or intentions which the observer believes are present, but does so infrequently and without much force or conviction about it; he doesn't act "defensive" in making the denial.
   c. Once or twice in the interview, the subject claims to have done something when all evidence points to the contrary.

2: Definite use of denial. The subject actively avoids inquiry about denied material, and there may also be extreme defensiveness about what is denied.
   a. In several instances the subject denies inquiries or suggestions about certain feelings, affective responses or intentions, to the point where it is clear the subject could not possibly be correct; e.g., a person describes being abused but denies any associated negative responses, and attempts to avoid further inquiry.
   b. The subject is hard to interview because he commonly responds with "no" to the interviewer's inquiries, at least some of which should yield more elaborate answers.
   c. The subject responds to the interviewer's questions or statements by denial accompanied by anger. Vehement attempts to avoid the topic may also follow. These may only occur once or twice, but they are usually disruptive to the flow of the interview. (E.g., Interviewer: "You must have felt sad." Subject: "Sad? No, that's not even relevant! I don't know why you would think that.")

GLOSSARY: DEFINITIONS OF DEFENSE MECHANISMS

Neurotic Denial (Minor Denial)

The subject actively denies that a feeling, behavioral response, or intention (regarding the past or present) is or was not present, even though its presence is considered more than likely by the observer. No delusional content is present in the denial. The subject is thus blind to both the ideational and emotional content of what is denied.

Projection

In nondelusional projection the subject disavows his own feelings, intentions or experience, but in addition makes a point of attributing them to others, usually others by whom the subject feels threatened in some way.

Hypochondriasis

Hypochondriasis involves the repetitious use of a complaint or series of complaints in which the subject ostensibly asks for help. However, covert feelings of hostility or resentment toward others are expressed simultaneously by the subject's rejection of the suggestions, advice, and so forth, that others offer. The complaints may consist of either somatic concerns or life problems. Either type of complaint is followed by a "help-rejecting complainer" response to whatever help is offered.

Passive Aggression

Passive aggression is characterized by the venting of hostile or resentful feelings in an indirect, veiled, and unassertive manner toward others. The use of the passive-aggressive defense often occurs when someone makes demands for independent action or performance by the subject or when someone disappoints the subject's wish or sense of entitlement to be taken care of, regardless of whether the subject has made this wish known. The defense is commonly found in the person who does everything "with a chip on his shoulder."

Acting Out

Acting out involves the immediate expression of feelings, wishes, or impulses in uncontrolled behavior with apparent disregard for personal or social consequences. It usually occurs in response to interpersonal events with significant people in the subject's life, such as parents, authority figures, friends, and lovers.

This definition is broader than the original concept of acting-out transference feelings or wishes that occur during psychotherapy. It includes behavior arising both within and outside of the transference relationship. It is not synonymous with "bad behavior," although acting out often involves socially disruptive or self-destructive behavior.

Fantasy

Fantasy denotes the use of daydreaming as either a pretense of dealing with or solving external problems, or as a way of expressing and satisfying one's feelings and desires. While the subject may be aware of the "I'm just pretending" quality of his use of fantasy, nonetheless, it may be the closest that he ever comes to expressing or gratifying his need for satisfying interpersonal relationships.

Splitting of Self-Images

In splitting of self-images, the subject demonstrates contradictory views, expectations, and feelings about himself which he cannot reconcile into one coherent whole. The self-images are divided into polar opposites: at a given time the subject's awareness is limited to those aspects of the self having the same emotional feeling tone. He sees himself in "black or white" terms. At one point in time the subject either believes he himself has good attributes, that he is loving, powerful, worthy, or correct and has good feelings, or he believes the opposite, that he is bad, hateful, angry, destructive, weak, powerless, worthless, or always wrong and has only negative feelings about himself. The subject cannot experience himself as a more realistic mixture of both positive and negative attributes. Moreover, the switch from experiencing the self exclusively in one polar feeling tone to experiencing the opposite feeling tone is unpredictable.

When the subject uses splitting, he cannot believe and integrate anything of an opposite feeling tone that contradicts the view he immediately experiences. Self-images with similar meanings stick together; they exclude contradictory self-images from emotional awareness, although not necessarily from cognitive awareness.

Splitting of Others' Images

In splitting of others' images (object images), the subject demonstrates that his views, expectations, and feelings about others are contradictory and that he cannot reconcile these differences to form realistic and coherent views of others. Object images are divided into polar opposites, such that the subject can only see one emotional aspect or side of the object at a time. Objects are experienced in black or white terms. At one time an object will seem to have only such traits as being loving, powerful, worthy, nurturant, and kind, with no attributes of opposite emotional significance. At another time the same object may be seen as bad, hateful, angry, destructive, rejecting, or worthless, and then the subject is incapable of seeing any positive attributes. In discussions, the subject commonly talks about some individuals in all positive terms and other individuals in all negative terms, as if the world were split into good and evil camps. The switch from experiencing an object as good to experiencing it as bad is unpredictable.

Splitting is revealed in two major ways. The subject may initially describe an object wholly in one way but later describe the same object in opposite ways. Second, the subject may describe several objects all in the same way, and describe a different group of objects in the opposite way. In the latter instance, the subject does not talk about a single object in contradictory ways. Rather each object is simply lumped with other objects into a good or bad, positive or negative camp.

When the subject uses splitting of object images, he cannot believe and integrate anything that does not match his immediate experience of and feeling about a given object. All of the attributes with the same feeling tone are highlighted, and contradictory views, expectations, or feelings about the object are excluded from emotional awareness, although not necessarily from cognitive awareness.

Mood Incongruent Denial (Manic Denial/Depressive Denial)

In this form of denial, the subject denies that his past feelings about a topic are contradictory to the present feelings, even though the contradiction is clear to the observer. The subject's present mood or feelings cast their shadow onto his past: he does not allow that he ever felt differently than he does at present about something in his own life. Mood incongruent denial should only be inferred when there is reasonable evidence from the subject's history that his present mood is obscuring the truth about his past feelings.

This defense tends to cut a wide swath through the subject's history. Many unrelated and varied emotional reactions are colored by the present feeling tone, whether positive or negative. When the subject is euphoric or elated, the defense is commonly called manic denial. The same defense operates, however, when the subject colors his past with a depressive hue, thereby negating what the interviewer can reasonably infer were positive experience.

Bland Denial

Bland denial is demonstrated by the subject's failure either to recognize or to react to contradictions in the self-report of his own actions, feelings, experience, or beliefs, when the interviewer points out such contradictions. The subject either fails to recognize the contradiction or fails to recognize the emotional significance of it. Rather than becoming embarrassed or distressed when confronted with the contradictions, the subject merely shrugs them off, ignores them, or doesn't seem to care to resolve the contradictions. Bland denial is generally seen only in response to direct questioning or confrontation by others.

Projective Identification

In projective identification the subject has an affect or impulse that he finds unacceptable and projects onto someone else, as if it were really the other person who originated the affect or impulse. However, the subject does not disavow what is projected—unlike the situation in simple projection—but remains fully aware of it and simply misattributes it as a justifiable reaction to the other person. Hence, the subject eventually admits his affect or impulse but believes it to be a reaction to those same feelings and impulses in others. The subject does not recognize that it was he himself who originated the projected material.

This defense is seen most clearly in a lengthy interchange in which the subject initially projects his feelings but later experiences his original feelings as reactions to the other. Paradoxically, the subject often arouses the very feelings in others that he at first mistakenly believed to be present in those others. It is then difficult to clarify who did what to whom first.

Primitive Idealization

In the defense of primitive idealization, the subject describes real or alleged relationships to others (including institutions, belief systems, etc.) who are powerful, revered, important, etc. This usually serves as a source of gratification as well as protection from feelings of powerlessness, unimportance, worthlessness, and the like. The defense accomplishes a sort of alchemy of worthiness by association.

Omnipotence

Omnipotence is a defense in which the subject makes claim to unrealistic powers, influence, inflated worth, etc. This most commonly allows the subject to deal with fears of powerlessness, worthlessness, and the like, which are minimized although obvious to others. It is different from reaction formation in that the minimized feelings are more obvious to the outsider, and the sense of power displayed is often more unrealistic or even childlike.

Devaluation

Devaluation refers to the use of derogatory, sarcastic, or other negative statements about oneself or others, which the subject commonly employs to fend off wishes to have his needs met or disappointment when they go unfulfilled. The negative comments about others usually cover up a certain sense of vulnerability or worthlessness, which the subject experiences vis-à-vis expressing his own wishes and meeting his own needs. Unlike the situation in projection, the subject does not dwell upon his object but rather dismisses each devalued object as he utters the negative description.

Repression

Repression is a defense that protects the subject from being aware of what he is experiencing. The subject may experience a particular affect, impulse, or desire, but the actual recognition of it—that is, of the idea associated with it—remains out of awareness. While the emotional elements are clearly present and experienced, the cognitive elements remain outside of consciousness.

When repression is in use, the subject has feelings and impulses that he fails to recognize, while similarly failing to recognize the situation or the object (person) that may evoke them. Unaware of why his impulses and feelings are at play, the subject expresses them unchanged or alters them by using an additional defense.

For instance, an urge to hit somebody that is repressed may be further altered by displacement, resulting in a temper tantrum by the subject over some minor annoyance.

Since repression plays a role that frequently leads to the operation of other defenses, it is important to rate repression in the present scale only when it stands by itself, not when it is used in immediate tandem with other specific defenses. Hence, repression, as it is measured by this scale, is a narrower, more delimited concept than that which appears throughout much of psychodynamic literature.

Dissociation

In the defense of dissociation, a particular affect or impulse operates in the subject's life out of normal awareness. The subject may be dimly aware that something unusual takes place at such times but full acknowledgment that his own affect or impulses are being expressed is not made. It may result in a loss of function or in uncharacteristic behavior.

Dissociated material is commonly experienced as too threatening, too conflict-laden, or too anxiety-provoking (e.g., recollection of a trauma) to be allowed into awareness and fully acknowledged by the subject. Dissociations that involve crime, or episodes of acting-out behavior for which the subject claims amnesia, need to be differentiated from lying.

Displacement

Displacement involves expressing an affect, impulse, or action toward a person (or other object) that holds some similarity to the original object that actually aroused the affect, etc. The affect, impulse, or whatever is fully acknowledged but misdirected to a less conflictual target. The person using displacement may or may not be aware that the emotion expressed toward the displaced object was really meant for someone else.

Reaction Formation

In reaction formation an original impulse or affect is deemed unacceptable by the subject, and an unconscious substitution is made. Feelings, impulses, and behaviors of opposite emotional tone are substituted for the original ones. The observer does not see the alteration per se but only the end product. It differs, therefore, from undoing, wherein the observer sees both opposites alternate without a resolution.

Reaction formation is reasonably inferred when a subject reacts to an event with an emotion opposite in tone to the usual feelings evoked in people. It is clearest in examples where caring and concern are substituted for anger or fear toward those who act against the subject.

Isolation

In the defense of isolation, the subject loses touch with the feelings associated with a given idea (e.g., a traumatic event) while remaining aware of the cognitive elements of it (e.g., descriptive details). Only affect is lost or detached, while the idea is conscious. It is the converse of repression, where the affect is retained but the idea is detached and unrecognized.

Sometimes affect can be detached temporarily from its associated idea. The affect is felt later without association to the original experience and idea. Instead, there is an intervening neutral interval between cognizance of the idea and experience of the associated affects.

Intellectualization

Intellectualization is a defense against affects or impulses in which the idea representing the affect or impulse is kept conscious and expressed as a generalization (not uncommonly expressed by the subject in the third person), while the affect or impulse itself is thereby detached. The felt quality of emotions is lost, as is the urge in any impulse. The cognitive elements remain conscious, although in generalized or impersonal terms.

One does not have to be bright or especially intelligent to use intellectualization. It is simply a cognitive strategy for minimizing the felt importance of problems in one's affective life.

Rationalization

Rationalization involves the substitution of a plausible reason for a given action by or impulse in the subject when a more self-serving motive is evident to the observer. The subject is usually unaware or minimally aware of his true underlying motive; instead, he sees only the substituted, more socially acceptable reason for the action. The subject's reasons commonly have nothing to do with any personal satisfaction and thus disguise his real impulse or motive, although any related affect may still show.

This defense is a first cousin to lying, and it may be difficult to distinguish whether someone is lying (a fully conscious act) or rationalizing.

Undoing

In this defense a subject expresses an affect or impulse or commits an action that makes him feel guilty or anxious. He then deals with this by expressing the opposite affect, impulse, or action. In conversation the subject's statements are immediately followed by qualifications bearing the opposite meaning from the original statement. To the observer this coupling of statement with contradictory statement may make it difficult to see what the subject's primary feeling or intention really is.

Misdeeds may be followed by acts of reparation for the intended object of the misdeed. The subject appears compelled to erase or undo his original action.

Affiliation

Affiliation involves dealing with emotional conflict and internal or external stressors by turning to others for help or support. By affiliating with others, the individual can confide, share problems, and feel less alone or isolated with a conflict or problem. This may also result in receiving advice or concrete help. It does not imply trying to make someone else responsible for dealing with one's own problems, nor does it imply coercing someone to help. Affili-ation is not shown simply by belonging to an organization (e.g., church, social club, AA) but by the give and take around conflicts and problems that occurs in the context of sharing or belonging to an organization.

Anticipatory Problem Solving

Anticipatory problem solving (anticipation) is a way of dealing with emotional conflicts and internal or external stressors by considering realistic alternative solutions or by anticipating emo-tional reactions to problems or conflicts. It involves doing some-thing to help before the problem occurs.

Suppression

Suppression deals with emotional conflict and internal or exter-nal stressors by voluntarily avoiding thinking about disturbing problems, wishes, feelings, or experiences temporarily. This may entail putting things out of one's mind until the right time to deal with them: it is postponing not procrastinating. Suppression may also entail avoiding thinking about something at the time because it would distract from engaging in another activity which one must do (e.g., not dwelling on tangential problems in order to deal with one pressing problem). The individual can call the sup-pressed material back to conscious attention readily, since it is not forgotten.

Self-Observation

The individual who uses self-observation deals with emotional conflicts and internal or external stressors by reflecting on his or her own thoughts, feelings, motivation, and behavior. This defense allows the individual to grow and adapt better as he deals with stress. In interpersonal situations the person is able to "see himself as others see him," and he may as a result understand better other people's reactions to him.

Self-Assertion

Self-assertion is a way of dealing with emotional conflict and internal or external stressors by expressing one's feelings and thoughts directly in order to achieve goals. Self-assertion is not coercive or indirect and manipulative. The goal or purpose of the self-assertive behavior is usually made clear to all parties affected by it.

Humor

Humor deals with emotional conflict and internal or external stressors by emphasizing the amusing or ironic aspects of the conflict or stressor. Humor tends to relieve the tension around conflict in a way that allows everyone to share in it, and it is not at one person's expense, as with derisive or cutting remarks. An element of self-observation or truth is often involved.

Altruism

The individual who uses altruism deals with emotional conflicts and internal or external stressors over fulfilling his own needs by dedication to fulfilling the needs of others. This is to be rated as present only when there is a demonstrable, strong functional relationship between the subject's feelings and response pattern. By using altruism, the individual receives some partial gratification either vicariously or from others' responses. The subject is usually aware of the personal needs or feelings that underlie his actions.

Sublimation

Sublimation is a defense against emotional conflicts or internal or external stressors in which the individual channels potentially maladaptive feelings or impulses into socially acceptable behavior. This defense is to be rated as present only when a strong functional relationship can be demonstrated between the feelings and response pattern. Classic examples of the use of sublimation are sports and games used to channel angry impulses, or artistic creation that expresses conflicted feelings, but the connection to a conflict must be evident.

V. Glossary of Defenses of Hauser and Colleagues[1]

ACTING OUT

Acting out refers to the behavioral expression of an unconscious wish or impulse in order to avoid the affect which would accompany its conscious recognition. Acting out may occur through the omission of a normally adjustive, appropriate behavior; or it may include the use of physical actions (such as overeating), delinquent, antisocial, or impulsive acts, and "tempers" to avoid awareness of feelings.

ALTRUISM

Altruism involves the surrender of direct gratification of needs in favor of vicarious satisfaction gained through service to others. Altruistic activities include philanthropy, well-repaid services, and open giving of oneself and one's time in an interview. Openness or talkativeness in the interview does not by itself constitute evidence of altruism, although it may be suggestive. To rate a subject as altruistic from the interview behavior there should be clear indications that the person intends to be helpful to or considerate of the interviewer and/or the abstract others who may gain benefit from the research.

Altruism differs from *projection* and *acting out* in that it provides real, not imaginary, benefits to others; from *reaction formation* in that the individual redirects instinctual gratifications rather than opposing them; and from *asceticism* in that it substitutes indirect gratification for renunciation.

---

[1]Authors of this Glossary are Alan M. Jacobson, M.D.; William Beardslee, M.D.; Stuart T. Hauser, M.D., Ph.D.; Gil Noam, Dipl. Psych.; Sally I. Powers, Ed.D.; and Elizabeth Gelfand, Ed.D.

ASCETICISM

Asceticism aims at the elimination or avoidance of pleasurable experience and is directed against all consciously perceived physical enjoyment. Gratification comes from renunciation of needs and pleasures; hence biological or sensual satisfactions are forbidden, whereas nonsensual joy is countenanced. Asceticism may be part of an ethical, religious, or moral concern, and one may find a moralistic tone present in the judgments of self and others.

AVOIDANCE

Avoidance entails an active "turning away" from conflict-laden thoughts, objects, feelings, or experiences. The avoidance can take many forms, including leaving a distressing situation, walking away from a discussion, closing the eyes, or refusing to talk about something. With avoidance there is an evasion of what one feels to be conflictual; with denial there is more likely a lack of awareness of the disturbing stimuli or events.

DENIAL

Denial involves the automatic refusal to acknowledge painful or disturbing aspects of inner or outer reality. At the low end of the scale denial is evidenced by minor lapses in awareness, and by efforts at minimizing discomfort and looking for the good in difficult situations. At the high end, external reality is denied: "I am not in the hospital; this is my country club." In mid-range, the painful or frightening import of events or perceptions is denied, although the evidence itself is acknowledged: "This cough has nothing to do with my cigarette smoking."

Denial contrasts with *repression*, which allows the affect surrounding a conflict to be experienced without awareness of the content; and with *suppression*, which entails the conscious or semiconscious decision to postpone but not to forget or avoid a painful reality. Denial's effectiveness may be enhanced through exaggeration, negation, and fantasy formation.

DISPLACEMENT

Displacement refers to the purposeful (albeit unconscious) redirection of feelings toward a safer or less important object than the person or situation arousing the feelings or impulses. The feelings remain the same, but their object is changed. Displacement involves the discharge of emotions, often angry or erotic, onto things, animals, or people perceived as less dangerous by the individual than those with whom the feelings were originally evoked.

INTELLECTUALIZATION

Intellectualization refers to thinking as a special and limited variety of doing; it is a mode of controlling affects and impulses by thinking them instead of experiencing the feelings associated with them. The person employing intellectualization uses the thinking process defensively, as a substitute for and protection against emotion and impulse. As a result, he or she emphasizes reason, devoid of affect, and tends to give blandly abstract, esoteric, or logical explanations of internal and external conditions. Intellectualization differs from *rationalization*, which is justification of irrational behavior through clichés, stories, and pat explanations.

PROJECTION

Projection involves the unconscious rejection of one's own unacceptable thoughts, traits, feelings, or wishes, and the attribution of them to other people. It is the perception and treatment of certain inner impulses, affects, and thoughts as if they were outside the self, as a way of making awareness of them tolerable. The rejected elements may be thoughts or feelings, wishes to do things, or criticisms.

Projection may be expressed in severe prejudice, in rejection of intimacy through unwarranted suspicion, in hypervigilance to danger, in injustice-collecting, or in exaggerated attention to others' sexual interests and behavior.

RATIONALIZATION

Rationalization refers to common-sense, utilitarian justifications of internal and external conditions. It is an effort to justify attitudes, beliefs, or behaviors that are irrational or otherwise unacceptable by the arbitrary application of a truth—a so-called "logical explanation"—or by the invention of a convincing fallacy. Rationalization is the unconsciously motivated and involuntary act of giving logical and believable explanations for irrational behaviors that have been prompted by unacceptable, unconscious wishes, or by the defenses used to cope with such wishes. It is the use of commonplace expressions and clichés to cover over puzzling, shameful, or embarrassing actions.

Rationalization differs from *intellectualization*—which also refers to the use of thoughts to handle unacceptable feelings and impulses—in that its aim is self-justification, rather than masking of painful affects.

REPRESSION

Repression consists of an unconsciously motivated forgetting or unawareness of external events or internal impulses, feelings, thoughts, or wishes. Although the repressed is not recognized consciously, its effects remain. Repression may be expressed in a variety of ways which will enable the rater to distinguish it from simple forgetting. When repression is expressed as forgetting, the persistence of the repressed in the unconscious may be sensed directly by the subject—in the feeling that one "ought" to know what has been forgotten, or even that one does know it "somehow," that it is "on the tip of the tongue"—or indirectly, when feeling is retained without memory. The forgetting associated with repression is unique in that it may be accompanied by a subjective sense that the repressed is not really forgotten; or by symbolic behavior, such as "accident-proneness," or shaking one's fist while saying that one is not angry. Repression may also be expressed as unawareness, e.g., unawareness that one's behavior is at odds with one's conscious intentions, or unawareness of the impact of one's behavior on others, or unawareness of how others will interpret one's actions, or restriction from awareness of certain fantasies or feelings.

Repression differs from *suppression* (which only postpones awareness) by effecting unconscious inhibition of thoughts, impulses, or memories; and from *denial* (in which awareness of inner or outer stimuli and of reactions to them is blocked) by restricting conscious awareness of thoughts, impulses, and memories, while leaving the feelings associated with them present. If a man wiped away his tears and said he would wait until later to cry, he would be utilizing suppression; if the weeping man said that he was not crying, he would be using denial; if he said that he didn't know why he was crying, he would be exhibiting repression.

SUPPRESSION

Suppression is the conscious or semiconscious decision to postpone (but *not* to avoid) paying attention to a conscious impulse, feeling, or conflict. It is a mechanism that temporarily removes a disturbing thought, feeling, fantasy, or impulse from awareness so that it can be dealt with at a more convenient or opportune time in the future. Suppression is differentiated from *rationalization*, where the point is to evade; and from *denial* and *repression*, which are attempts at permanent removal from awareness. The person utilizing suppression returns to the subject at a later time.

TURNING AGAINST THE SELF

This mechanism entails turning back upon the self an aggressive impulse directed against another person. Turning against the self is displacement onto oneself, the singular displacement of using oneself as the object. This means that the identity of the original object of hostility remains obscure, and sometimes the emotion itself remains outside conscious awareness. When hostility is turned inward on the self, the person may injure himself physically or in other ways—socially, financially, academically, professionally, etc. Certain procrastinations, failures, and provocative behaviors (including passive-aggressive ones) may be reflections of this mechanism. There must be not only evidence of self-destructive behavior but also evidence of previous hostility to another: getting in trouble per se does not indicate turning against the self.

OVERALL SUCCESS OF DEFENSES

This scale is a global rating of the effectiveness of the subject's defenses, and an overall measure of the subject's variety and flexibility of responses to internal and external stimuli. Optimal functioning allows for *both* protection against inappropriate breakthroughs of impulses, thoughts, and actions; and for emotional and cognitive richness through access to a wide range of feelings and fantasies.

CASE EXAMPLE: ASCETICISM

Asceticism aims at the elimination or avoidance of pleasurable experience and is directed against all consciously perceived physical enjoyment. Gratification comes from renunciation of needs and pleasures; hence biological or sensual satisfactions are forbidden, whereas nonsensual joy is countenanced. Asceticism may be part of an ethical, religious, or moral concern, and one may find a moralistic tone present in the judgments of self and others.

1. *Minimal:* The subject displays no interest in inhibiting pleasure-seeking; is not preoccupied with selfishness; is not critical of others for their sensuality; is almost disinhibited.
2. *Little:* The subject is not critical of others for excessive pleasures; is not preoccupied with the issue of satisfaction vs. renunciation; is almost neutral—not controlling but also not wild.
3. *Moderate:* The subject may eschew certain pleasures, such as drugs or sex, while advocating and enjoying others. S/he holds some "antipleasure" values but also engages in some sensually gratifying activities such as dancing and contact sports.

4. *Considerable:* The subject renounces many if not most physical pleasures. S/he has some areas of sensual satisfaction, but they are limited and closely monitored.
5. *Maximal:* The subject lives an extremely spartan existence, forswearing physical comfort and material display. S/he is concerned only with spiritual, intellectual, or esthetic satisfactions and finds bodily pleasures irrelevant and distasteful.

X: Cannot say

Rating 1: Minimal

The subject gets pleasure from immediate gratification. There is no second-guessing of animal pleasures, or guilt over getting what he wants even if it really does hurt someone else. He likes money in his pocket, and likes to spend it. "I'd have, like over a hundred dollars on me. And in two days, it would be gone. I'd buy pot, I'd buy mescaline—just to get a kick out of the stuff."

Rating 2: Little

The subject is not critical of others for enjoying pleasurable activities. She participates in sports and some mild amounts of drug and alcohol use for pleasure. On the other hand, she is quite capable of controlling these activities and limiting them to social occasions. She works hard in school and at sports, and derives pleasure from her accomplishments in these areas. While she gives no specific examples of renouncing pleasure for herself, or of criticizing others for their pleasures, neither does she give examples of a kind of wild, free pleasure or enjoyment for herself. Thus, by implication, she is not totally without asceticism and was rated as Little.

Another subject was rated a 2 because of the absence of descriptions of intense interest either in prohibiting pleasure or in seeking pleasure. For example, at no time does he deride others for membership in religious groups that are antipleasure, or criticize people for letting loose at parties. Rather, the transcript is devoid of criticisms in either direction. He does seem to have some fun at making money, although he uses the money for saving for the future rather than for giving himself pleasures now. He would be rated lower if there were examples of his using the money, or if he described a great deal of interest in occasions of pleasure such as drinking, drug-taking, or sexual activities. The transcript is, overall, generally neutral regarding asceticism.

Rating 3: Moderate

This adolescent evidences some criticism or renunciation of pleasure for herself and for others, yet also participates in some enjoyable peer activities. She derives satisfaction from "being good," and notes that at times she feels uncomfortable with kids her own age because "I think smoking pot and stuff like that is all right since it's way better than smoking cigarettes, but it's something that I don't want to do." On the other hand, she mentions that she would like to spend more time with certain of her friends, the kids who are "like her": who aren't into partying but who enjoy going to Harvard Square and tasting different foods, listening to street musicians, and playing touch football.

Rating 4: Considerable

This adolescent strongly criticizes the pleasure-seeking activities of her peers and sets herself apart from them: "I know 15-year-olds who smoke grass and hang around and start screaming and yelling. It's bad, it looks bad, and I don't want to be in that kind of group." Similarly, sexual activity is perceived as "doing things together; disgusting, perverted things." She is mistrustful of her peers who enjoy themselves socially at parties; she sees them as "loose and immature," and avoids them. A salient feature of the transcript is this subject's strong objection to sensual pleasure. She is, however, comfortable enjoying a good meal when she is hungry, or on a nature walk.

Rating 5: Maximal

The subject, a 17-year-old adolescent, has developed an ideology renouncing any form of worldly pleasure. He is highly critical of any form of materialism, such as spending money for clothes or other personal comforts. He is also opposed to any sexual intimacies, feeling that they detract from dedication to the spiritual life. He is very intolerant of people who are pleasure-seekers and feels that society should make it impossible to live comfortably. He feels that only the strengthening of body and soul through austerity makes life worth living.

VI. Bond's Defense Style Questionnaire (1984 Version)[1]

INSTRUCTIONS

This questionnaire consists of 88 statements, each of which is followed by a rating scale:

Strongly Disagree   1 2 3 4 5 6 7 8 9   Strongly Agree

Rate the degree to which you agree or disagree with each statement and write your rating from one to nine on the answer sheet.

Example: Montreal is a city in Canada.

Strongly Disagree   1 2 3 4 5 6 7 8 9   Strongly Agree

You would choose 9 and write 9 on the answer sheet beside the statement number.

*1. I get satisfaction from helping others and if this were taken away from me I would get depressed.
   Strongly Disagree   1 2 3 4 5 6 7 8 9   Strongly Agree
*2. People often call me a sulker.
   Strongly Disagree   1 2 3 4 5 6 7 8 9   Strongly Agree
*3. I'm able to keep a problem out of my mind until I have time to deal with it.
   Strongly Disagree   1 2 3 4 5 6 7 8 9   Strongly Agree

---

[1] Devised by Michael Bond, M.D. Scoring manual available from Dr. M. Bond, 4333 Côte Ste. Catherine Road, Montréal, Québec, Canada H3T 1E4
*Indicates the 67 items used by Vaillant in Chapter 5.

*4. I'm always treated unfairly.
   Strongly Disagree   1 2 3 4 5 6 7 8 9   Strongly Agree
*5. I work out my anxiety through doing something constructive
   and creative like painting or woodwork.
   Strongly Disagree   1 2 3 4 5 6 7 8 9   Strongly Agree
*6. Once in a while I put off until tomorrow what I ought to do
   today.
   Strongly Disagree   1 2 3 4 5 6 7 8 9   Strongly Agree
*7. I keep getting into the same type of frustrating situations and I
   don't know why.
   Strongly Disagree   1 2 3 4 5 6 7 8 9   Strongly Agree
*8. I'm able to laugh at myself pretty easily.
   Strongly Disagree   1 2 3 4 5 6 7 8 9   Strongly Agree
*9. I act like a child when I'm frustrated.
   Strongly Disagree   1 2 3 4 5 6 7 8 9   Strongly Agree
*10. I'm very shy about standing up for my rights with people.
   Strongly Disagree   1 2 3 4 5 6 7 8 9   Strongly Agree
*11. I am superior to most people I know.
   Strongly Disagree   1 2 3 4 5 6 7 8 9   Strongly Agree
*12. People tend to mistreat me.
   Strongly Disagree   1 2 3 4 5 6 7 8 9   Strongly Agree
*13. If someone mugged me and stole my money, I'd rather he'd
   be helped than punished.
   Strongly Disagree   1 2 3 4 5 6 7 8 9   Strongly Agree
*14. Once in a while I think of things too bad to talk about.
   Strongly Disagree   1 2 3 4 5 6 7 8 9   Strongly Agree
*15. Once in a while I laugh at a dirty joke.
   Strongly Disagree   1 2 3 4 5 6 7 8 9   Strongly Agree
*16. People say I'm like an ostrich with my head buried in the
   sand. In other words, I tend to ignore unpleasant facts as if
   they didn't exist.
   Strongly Disagree   1 2 3 4 5 6 7 8 9   Strongly Agree
*17. I stop myself from going all out in a competition.
   Strongly Disagree   1 2 3 4 5 6 7 8 9   Strongly Agree
*18. I often feel superior to people I'm with.
   Strongly Disagree   1 2 3 4 5 6 7 8 9   Strongly Agree

*19. Someone is robbing me emotionally of all I've got.
   Strongly Disagree   1 2 3 4 5 6 7 8 9   Strongly Agree

*20. I get angry sometimes.
   Strongly Disagree   1 2 3 4 5 6 7 8 9   Strongly Agree

*21. I often am driven to act impulsively.
   Strongly Disagree   1 2 3 4 5 6 7 8 9   Strongly Agree

*22. I'd rather starve than be forced to eat.
   Strongly Disagree   1 2 3 4 5 6 7 8 9   Strongly Agree

*23. I ignore danger as if I were Superman.
   Strongly Disagree   1 2 3 4 5 6 7 8 9   Strongly Agree

*24. I pride myself on my ability to cut people down to size.
   Strongly Disagree   1 2 3 4 5 6 7 8 9   Strongly Agree

*25. People tell me I have a persecution complex.
   Strongly Disagree   1 2 3 4 5 6 7 8 9   Strongly Agree

*26. Sometimes when I am not feeling well I am cross.
   Strongly Disagree   1 2 3 4 5 6 7 8 9   Strongly Agree

*27. I often act impulsively when something is bothering me.
   Strongly Disagree   1 2 3 4 5 6 7 8 9   Strongly Agree

*28. I get physically ill when things aren't going well for me.
   Strongly Disagree   1 2 3 4 5 6 7 8 9   Strongly Agree

*29. I'm a very inhibited person.
   Strongly Disagree   1 2 3 4 5 6 7 8 9   Strongly Agree

*30. I'm a real put-down artist.
   Strongly Disagree   1 2 3 4 5 6 7 8 9   Strongly Agree

*31. I do not always tell the truth.
   Strongly Disagree   1 2 3 4 5 6 7 8 9   Strongly Agree

*32. I withdraw from people when I feel hurt.
   Strongly Disagree   1 2 3 4 5 6 7 8 9   Strongly Agree

*33. I often push myself so far that other people have to set limits for me.
   Strongly Disagree   1 2 3 4 5 6 7 8 9   Strongly Agree

*34. My friends see me as a clown.
   Strongly Disagree   1 2 3 4 5 6 7 8 9   Strongly Agree

*35. I withdraw when I'm angry.
   Strongly Disagree   1 2 3 4 5 6 7 8 9   Strongly Agree

*36. I tend to be on my guard with people who turn out to be more friendly than I would have suspected.
Strongly Disagree   1 2 3 4 5 6 7 8 9   Strongly Agree

*37. I've got special talents that allow me to go through life with no problems.
Strongly Disagree   1 2 3 4 5 6 7 8 9   Strongly Agree

*38. Sometimes at elections I vote for men about whom I know very little.
Strongly Disagree   1 2 3 4 5 6 7 8 9   Strongly Agree

*39. I'm often late for appointments.
Strongly Disagree   1 2 3 4 5 6 7 8 9   Strongly Agree

*40. I work more things out in my daydreams than in my real life.
Strongly Disagree   1 2 3 4 5 6 7 8 9   Strongly Agree

*41. I'm very shy about approaching people.
Strongly Disagree   1 2 3 4 5 6 7 8 9   Strongly Agree

*42. I fear nothing.
Strongly Disagree   1 2 3 4 5 6 7 8 9   Strongly Agree

*43. Sometimes I think I'm an angel and other times I think I'm a devil.
Strongly Disagree   1 2 3 4 5 6 7 8 9   Strongly Agree

*44. I would rather win than lose in a game.
Strongly Disagree   1 2 3 4 5 6 7 8 9   Strongly Agree

*45. I get very sarcastic when I'm angry.
Strongly Disagree   1 2 3 4 5 6 7 8 9   Strongly Agree

*46. I get openly aggressive when I feel hurt.
Strongly Disagree   1 2 3 4 5 6 7 8 9   Strongly Agree

*47. I believe in turning the other cheek when someone hurts me.
Strongly Disagree   1 2 3 4 5 6 7 8 9   Strongly Agree

*48. I do not read every editorial in the newspaper every day.
Strongly Disagree   1 2 3 4 5 6 7 8 9   Strongly Agree

*49. I withdraw when I'm sad.
Strongly Disagree   1 2 3 4 5 6 7 8 9   Strongly Agree

*50. I'm shy about sex.
Strongly Disagree   1 2 3 4 5 6 7 8 9   Strongly Agree

*51. I always feel that someone I know is like a guardian angel.
Strongly Disagree   1 2 3 4 5 6 7 8 9   Strongly Agree

*52. My philosophy is, "Hear no evil, do no evil, see no evil."
Strongly Disagree   1 2 3 4 5 6 7 8 9   Strongly Agree

*53. As far as I'm concerned, people are either good or bad.
Strongly Disagree   1 2 3 4 5 6 7 8 9   Strongly Agree

*54. If my boss bugged me, I might make a mistake in my work or work more slowly so as to get back at him.
Strongly Disagree   1 2 3 4 5 6 7 8 9   Strongly Agree

*55. Everyone is against me.
Strongly Disagree   1 2 3 4 5 6 7 8 9   Strongly Agree

*56. I try to be nice to people I don't like.
Strongly Disagree   1 2 3 4 5 6 7 8 9   Strongly Agree

*57. I would be very nervous if an airplane in which I was flying lost an engine.
Strongly Disagree   1 2 3 4 5 6 7 8 9   Strongly Agree

*58. There is someone I know who can do anything and who is absolutely fair and just.
Strongly Disagree   1 2 3 4 5 6 7 8 9   Strongly Agree

*59. I can keep the lid on my feelings if it would interfere with what I'm doing if I were to let them out.
Strongly Disagree   1 2 3 4 5 6 7 8 9   Strongly Agree

*60. Some people are plotting to kill me.
Strongly Disagree   1 2 3 4 5 6 7 8 9   Strongly Agree

*61. I'm usually able to see the funny side of an otherwise painful predicament.
Strongly Disagree   1 2 3 4 5 6 7 8 9   Strongly Agree

*62. I get a headache when I have to do something I don't like.
Strongly Disagree   1 2 3 4 5 6 7 8 9   Strongly Agree

*63. I often find myself being very nice to people who by all rights I should be angry at.
Strongly Disagree   1 2 3 4 5 6 7 8 9   Strongly Agree

*64. There's no such thing as "finding a little good in everyone." If you're bad, you're all bad.
Strongly Disagree   1 2 3 4 5 6 7 8 9   Strongly Agree

*65. We should never get angry at people we don't like.
Strongly Disagree 1 2 3 4 5 6 7 8 9 Strongly Agree

*66. I am sure I get a raw deal from life.
Strongly Disagree 1 2 3 4 5 6 7 8 9 Strongly Agree

*67. I fall apart under stress.
Strongly Disagree 1 2 3 4 5 6 7 8 9 Strongly Agree

68. When I know that I will have to face a difficult situation, like an exam or a job interview, I try to imagine what it will be like and plan ways to cope with it.
Strongly Disagree 1 2 3 4 5 6 7 8 9 Strongly Agree

69. Doctors never really understand what is wrong with me.
Strongly Disagree 1 2 3 4 5 6 7 8 9 Strongly Agree

70. When someone close to me dies, I don't feel upset.
Strongly Disagree 1 2 3 4 5 6 7 8 9 Strongly Agree

71. After I fight for my rights, I tend to apologize for my assertiveness.
Strongly Disagree 1 2 3 4 5 6 7 8 9 Strongly Agree

72. Most of what happens to me is not my responsibility.
Strongly Disagree 1 2 3 4 5 6 7 8 9 Strongly Agree

73. When I'm depressed or anxious, eating makes me feel better.
Strongly Disagree 1 2 3 4 5 6 7 8 9 Strongly Agree

74. Hard work makes me feel better.
Strongly Disagree 1 2 3 4 5 6 7 8 9 Strongly Agree

75. My doctors are not able to help me really get over my problems.
Strongly Disagree 1 2 3 4 5 6 7 8 9 Strongly Agree

76. I'm often told that I don't show my feelings.
Strongly Disagree 1 2 3 4 5 6 7 8 9 Strongly Agree

77. I believe that people usually see more meaning in films, plays or books than is actually there.
Strongly Disagree 1 2 3 4 5 6 7 8 9 Strongly Agree

78. I have habits or rituals which I feel compelled to do or else something terrible will happen.
Strongly Disagree 1 2 3 4 5 6 7 8 9 Strongly Agree

79. I take drugs, medicine or alcohol when I'm tense.
Strongly Disagree 1 2 3 4 5 6 7 8 9 Strongly Agree

80. When I feel bad, I try to be with someone.
    Strongly Disagree   1 2 3 4 5 6 7 8 9   Strongly Agree
81. If I can predict that I'm going to be sad ahead of time, I can cope better.
    Strongly Disagree   1 2 3 4 5 6 7 8 9   Strongly Agree
82. No matter how much I complain, I never get a satisfactory response.
    Strongly Disagree   1 2 3 4 5 6 7 8 9   Strongly Agree
83. Often I find that I don't feel anything when the situation would seem to warrant strong emotions.
    Strongly Disagree   1 2 3 4 5 6 7 8 9   Strongly Agree
84. Sticking to the task at hand keeps me from feeling depressed or anxious.
    Strongly Disagree   1 2 3 4 5 6 7 8 9   Strongly Agree
85. I smoke when I'm nervous.
    Strongly Disagree   1 2 3 4 5 6 7 8 9   Strongly Agree
86. If I were in a crisis, I would seek out another person who had the same problem.
    Strongly Disagree   1 2 3 4 5 6 7 8 9   Strongly Agree
87. I cannot be blamed for what I do wrong.
    Strongly Disagree   1 2 3 4 5 6 7 8 9   Strongly Agree
88. If I have an aggressive thought, I feel the need to do something to compensate for it.
    Strongly Disagree   1 2 3 4 5 6 7 8 9   Strongly Agree